County Council

Libraries, books and more . . .

1 4 OCT 2008

CAllcr

2 6 MAY 2017

D1313168

Please return/renew this item by the last due date.
Library items may also be renewed by phone or
via our website.
www.cumbria.gov.uk/libraries

CLIC

Ask for a CLIC password

THE
FOOTBALLER OF LOOS

A STORY OF THE 1ST BATTALION
LONDON IRISH RIFLES IN THE FIRST WORLD WAR

ED HARRIS

The
History
Press

Who is going to benefit by the carnage, save the rats which feed now as they have never fed before? What has brought about this turmoil, this tragedy that cuts the heart of friend and foe alike? Why have the millions of men come here from all corners of Europe to hack and slay one another?
Patrick MacGill, *The Great Push*

An image of Loos by Lady Butler (1916) reproduced courtesy of the London Irish Rifles Regimental Association.

First published 2009

The History Press
The Mill, Brimscombe Port
Stroud, Gloucestershire, GL5 2QG
www.thehistorypress.co.uk

British Library Cataloguing in Publication Data.
A catalogue record for this book is available from the British Library.

ISBN 978 0 7524 5166 4

Printed in Great Britain

Contents

List of Illustrations

Foreword

On 3 November 2007 the officers, soldiers and former members of D (London Irish Rifles) Company, The London Regiment, dined together at their TA Centre, Connaught House, Camberwell, South London, in commemoration of the Battle of Loos. It is a tradition of the Company annually to commemorate the battle on the weekend closest to the anniversary of its start on 25 September but, 92 years on, the dinner was postponed to allow those of the Company who had served on an operational tour in Afghanistan with 'Somme Company' of the London Regiment, to be present on their return.

The Battle of Loos remains central in the history and consciousness of the London Irish Rifles. It is the occasion that those who still bear the name of the Regiment that was raised in 1908 and provided two battalions in both the First and Second World Wars, remember and honour their dead. The story of the Footballer of Loos still inspires young and old soldiers alike and is the lifeblood of what is known as Regimental spirit.

In this excellent book, which Ed Harris has sub-titled 'a story', the history of the 1st Battalion's contribution to the Battle of Loos has been meticulously researched and has been personalised by an account of the life of Rifleman Edwards. All the misery, futility, stupidity, bravery and glory of the Great War are illustrated in these pages. It will be set reading for members of the London Irish Rifles and a treat for military historians and social historians alike.

Brigadier Digby O'Lone MSc
Honorary Colonel the London Irish Rifles

Acknowledgements

My thanks and appreciation to all the staff at the following archives, museums and collections: St Dunstan's, Westminster Reference Library, Michael Ball, Head of the Department of Printed Books and the wonderfully helpful lady on duty in the reading room at the National Army Museum on the morning of 10 March 2006. Aldershot Military Museum, Juliet Chaplin MBE, Branch Support Officer, and Louise Shaw, Soldiers, Sailors, Airman and Families Association; Joyce Carlyle, Administrative Officer, Historical Disclosures, Army Personnel Centre, Glasgow; British Museum Newspaper Library, Colindale, National Football Museum, Kensington & Chelsea Local Studies, Richard Callaghan, Royal Military Police Museum, Imperial War Museum, Hammersmith and Fulham Local Studies, Royal Borough of Kensington and Chelsea Register Office, London Borough of Richmond upon Thames Local Studies and Nicholas Malton, Records Manager, NSPCC Library and Information Service.

Grateful thanks to those who gave permission to use their photographs and illustrations in this volume. Every effort has been made to contact the known and perceived copyright holders, their assigns or heirs. The author and publishers will be happy to acknowledge any copyright holders not listed on reprint.

Thanks also to Ron Knight; to Michael Gavaghan for the benefit of his experience in the eventual production of this book and to Paul Reed, The Old Front Line; to Tim Plumb for generous access to his picture library and Anne Williamson, manager of the Henry Williamson Literary Estate. Special thanks to Captain Bob Keating, Tony Robinson and A. Roberts of the London Irish Rifles who stoically managed my requests to pillage the Regimental Museum, especially Nigel Wilkinson for his interest, encouragement and editorial input. Much thanks also to Brigadier O'Lone, Honorary Colonel, London Irish Rifles, for finding the time to pen such an encouraging foreword.

Introduction

Moving back into the house where she was born and raised after an absence of twenty years, my wife brought down from the cluttered roof space a small brown suitcase wrapped in a coat of grey dust. I was charged with forcing its small, insubstantial lock, which I did. Inside was a neatly folded Union flag, a small leather truncheon, a policeman's whistle dated 1915, a tin of medals and a large brown envelope containing a collection of newspaper clippings, mostly undated and featuring the exploit of a First World War Tommy they called The Footballer of Loos.

'Twenty Years Ago Today' exclaimed the headline of one fragile cutting, with the sub-heading 'Loos, and the early-morning football match there'. This came from a two-part series about 'the Saturday afternoon soldiers', wherein the *London Evening News* for 17 Tuesday 1959 recalled the day when the London Irish Rifles 'kicked a football into battle'. Other clippings from unidentifiable newspapers marked the death of Frank Edwards, the former London Irish rifleman who 'kicked off' the Battle of Loos. One in particular trumpeted the headline: 'Old soldiers go to war again', in what was clearly an age-old question as to whether or not Frank Edwards was or was not the Tommy they called The Footballer of Loos.

Frank Edwards was my wife's grandfather and she had talked about him, although I had never really made the association from my childhood of the image of a football booted over the top prior to a great charge. A military swagger stick had always rested by the fireplace in the room where Frank ended his days, next to the German officer's sword allegedly liberated from the 'Kaiser's Palace', but it was only with his famous exploit in print that the story came alive. Clearly there was a time when Frank Edwards was the man perceived as having 'kicked his way to glory'. The manner in which he 'made history', as one cutting had it, would doubtless be well documented, or so I thought. Alas, the first internet search for 'The Footballer of Loos' several years ago was met with pages devoted to the alleged antics of PR Girl Rebecca Loos and footballer David Beckham. 'The Battle of Loos' itself fared little better compared to Ypres, the Somme, Passendael, Verdun and the other horrific episodes of mass slaughter in the first global conflict of the twentieth century.

In a nutshell, the Battle of Loos began on 25 September and officially ended on 8 October 1915. In the first two hours more British soldiers died than did the total number of casualties in all three services on D-Day 1944, on both sides. Loos was the scene of the first 'Big Push' by the British Army on the Western Front and where it employed asphyxiating gas for the first time. Failure to bring up the reserves countered the initial success and lost a faltering commander-in-chief his job. The Battle of Loos fast became a cliché for all the ills of the First World War and was largely consigned to the footnotes of its history.

In 1976, military historian Philip Warner wrote *The Battle of Loos*. The first examination of any consequence before that was in Alan Clark's highly controversial *The Donkeys*, written in the 1960s. Warner felt that it was time for a comprehensive account of the actions at Loos and so mustered what first hand accounts could be drawn from survivors of the battle. Armed with more than 150 replies from veterans and with unprecedented access to the diaries of Sir John French, he believed such a combination would allow for a reconstruction of the battle 'as it appeared to the men who fought it'. While it does contain a wealth of personal recollections, expert criticism comes from the lack of core debate surrounding what history records as the failure at Loos. Niall Cherry's *Most Unfavourable Ground*, published in 2005, essentially concludes that all the chaos experienced by the British at Loos was as a result of a series of adverse external factors and not entirely the fault of the generals, as Alan Clark and others would have it. In 2006 Gordon Corrigan used contemporary accounts, war diaries and his own personal knowledge of the ground to chart the course of the battle in *Loos 1915: The Unwanted Battle* to assess the competence of commanders and the capabilities of men and equipment in what was effectively the last gasp of the old regular British Army. Then there is military historian, Nick Lloyd, who has produced what is generally regarded as the definitive study in *Loos 1915*, again drawing upon available eyewitness accounts, war diaries and post-battle reports to provide what he describes as a full account of what occurred once the main assault began on the morning of 25 September 1915. None of these authors, however, spend much time concentrating on the Battalions of the London Division, of which the 1st London Irish was afforded 'the honour' of leading the charge, begun by following Frank Edwards' football.

In any account of Loos the casual observer can be forgiven for thinking that the battle was essentially a Scottish affair, a notion that Nick Lloyd does little to dispel, concentrating chiefly on the heroic assault of the 15th (Scottish) Division, although this is not something unique to him. From the illustrated weekly periodicals of the day through to Lloyd's contemporaries, the Scots loom large at Loos in picture and in print, and so they should. Like any killing field of the Great War, the Battle of Loos is steeped in bloody disaster and it is not the business of this account to question the achievements of any of those brave souls who took part. Rather it is the business of this investigation to explore why historical references to the 47th Division in general and to the London Irish Rifles specifically are as rare as they are clipped. Many other eyewitness accounts exist, almost all of which are missing from earlier studies. Captain C. J. C. Street, OBE MC, for example, was a forward observation officer with the Royal Garrison Artillery Reserve. In his memoirs *With the Guns*, published in 1916, he recalls:

> Of those who took part in the struggle agree, the 47th Division, London Territorials all of them, the heroes of the day, but of whose performances, because less showy, little has been heard, had by 9.30a.m. surmounted a series of obstacles, the storming of any one of which would have earned them lasting fame. Like a tide they poured over the western end of the dreaded Double Crassier, utterly regardless of withering machine-gun fire, and swept to the attack of the walled cemetery that stands to the south-west of Loos. From here, after a titanic struggle, they dislodged the strong party of its defenders, and, gaining fresh impetus from the check, irresistibly fought their way through the outskirts of the village, in which every point of vantage was held against them, right up to its heart, the mine buildings that cluster at the foot of the Pylons. This fortress they stormed and won, and the rush of their assault carried them on its crest over the Loos Crassier – another high embankment of refuse and slag – over the exposed surface of the plain, into the copse that stretches westward from Loos Chalk Pit. Here at last for a while they rested … May the great city be for ever proud of the achievements of her sons this day, the thousand forgotten deeds of heroism of which her ears will never hear!

The official record paints a somewhat different picture. The 47th was favoured by higher ground, so that the poison gas, first used by the British, would roll more satisfactorily into the enemy in its sector than it did elsewhere. It faced enemy rifle and machine-gun fire that was inaccurate and once the gas cylinders were spent, slackened off considerably. The Londoners also enjoyed comprehensive pre-battle preparations and more effective artillery support. Division Brigadier-General, A. A. Montgomery, noted that their mission was 'far easier' than the tasks allotted other divisions deployed further north that were required to make all-out attacks. In his opinion, because the limited objective proved easier, did not make it the right decision, nor did the failure of the all-out attack prove to be a mistake. The latter failed because of a 'faulty method of execution, and not the selection of the wrong form of objective', whatever that means. Semantics aside, the 47th succeeded in the taking of its objectives with minimal casualties, and perhaps it is because of this its achievements sit uneasily outside of the first mass slaughter of British troops on the Western Front.

It might be argued that the 1st Battalion London Irish Rifles was the victim of its own success at Loos, its memory largely confined to the Mess Room. On the tenth anniversary of the battle in 1925, the grand Wembley Searchlight Tattoo was devoted to the action on the Somme a year before its actual anniversary, forcing the London Irish Rifles to defer commemorations of Loos to the following year with a Torchlight Tattoo at the regiment's head-quarters in Chelsea. Frank Edwards, then a sergeant in the Military Police, returned to his old unit to re-enact the moment he sent a football flying over the parapet towards the Germans lines. The 20th anniversary of the battle (in 1935) was more widely commemorated in a number of newspapers, particularly a feature article written for the London *Evening News* by S. F. Major, formerly a Second Lieutenant in the 1st Battalion London Irish Rifles. In it he laid out the 'Irish' action at Loos and the pivotal role of the 47th Division. Frank Edwards, as the 'mad footballer', was subsequently invited by the BBC to talk of his famous exploit.

Where this account of the Battle of Loos deviates from the few published histories to date is in its focus on the lead battalion of the 47th Division, the 1st Battalion London Irish Rifles, and in particular on the journey of Frank Edwards from volunteer to veteran. During the research process hard evidence proved as sparse as it was inaccessible. The source materials, where they exist, are hidden in published memoirs, some long forgotten or only briefly in the public domain. Personal correspondence is like the newspaper reports, fragmentary and tantalisingly illusive. In November 1915, despite the draconian censorship laws of the war years, the popular *Weekly Despatch* published the first and only full account of the London Irish at Loos, courtesy of an anonymous rifleman returned home wounded. In it, the football exploit is recorded, although the name of Frank Edwards is not. Its veracity is muddled with intention as a result of its publisher's quest to soothe the troublesome 'Irish Question', which carried into the war a residual anti-Irish prejudice long open to manipulation as a political force in British politics. Germans troops would call out across No Man's Land, wanting to know the names of regiments. When asked the same question themselves, they liked to answer provocatively: 'We're a battalion of Irish rifles', as if to imply that the Irish regiments were disloyal to England and not to be trusted. To counter this perception, a highly controlled British press took every opportunity to celebrate the Irish regiments and their place in the doings of Empire, which begs the question why the success of the London Irish at Loos was not widely exploited.

Within the strict censorship laws in place at the time, there is much in Captain Street's account that bravely bucks the trend. Unlike the many other personal accounts and memoirs of the war that filled the bookshelves between 1914 and 1919, Street's only concession to the prevailing authoritarianism was in his use of the non-de-plume F.O.O. (forward observation officer). Street, it later transpired, was also Henry Williamson's main authorial source for the Battle of Loos in his acclaimed novel *A Fox Under My Clock*. While Street's account is strictly limited to that of an observer reporting back to those behind the lines, Williamson's account of Loos is regarded as one of the finest illustrations of history by fiction ever written. But due to his heavy reliance on the Official History, the London Territorials enjoy nothing more than a passing reference. The prolific inter-war crime writer, Geoffrey Belton Cobb, however, actually served with the London Irish Rifles and like Frank Edwards was wounded at the Battle of Loos. He returned to England where he wrote *Stand To Arms!* under his own name, but casting himself as Allan Webb, late of the fictitious Eatonshire Regiment. Only the self-professed 'Navvie' poet and writer, Patrick MacGill, a stretcher bearer with the London Irish Rifles, writes openly of his own experience, the London Territorials and their place in Loos history. In *The Great Push*, he evokes the true calamity of the trenches and the futility of the murderous war, drawing on the footballing episode as a sprinkling of humanity. Other writers and journalists such as Philip Gibbs and James Hall also bucked the trend and took on Kitchener's propaganda machine to breathe life into that about Loos which has subsequently become lost in translation.

While the body of evidence drawn from the customary sources is small, it becomes highly significant within the context of the history of the 1st Battalion London Irish Rifles in the Great War, which lay undisturbed in the vaults of the Imperial War Museum since the 1970s. Former Second Lieutenant S. F. Major was charged in the 1920s with writing it up, a task he did not complete until half a century later when his son had it privately bound and presented to the Museum. From all of this emerges a fresh perspective on Loos, embracing the exploit of a football-mad stationer's assistant called Frank Edwards who, three days after Britain had declared war on Germany, took himself along to the Duke of York's Headquarters in Chelsea to sign up with 1st Battalion 18th (County of London) Regiment, Territorial Force, London Irish Rifles. Earl Kitchener's call for 100,000 volunteers on 11 August was answered in two weeks. A fortnight after that and the situation in France led to a call for a further 100,000 volunteers, one of whom would add another twist of fate wherein Frank's audacious act would be overshadowed by the greatest loss on the battlefield in British military history.

In September 1914, the first of 84,000 young men passed through the gates of Kingston-upon-Thames Barracks to sign up with the 8th (Service) Battalion, East Surreys. Come the spring of 1915, both it and the 1st Battalion London Irish Rifles were deemed ready, prepared and sent to France as part of Kitchener's New Army. By autumn, the 7th and 8th Battalions East Surreys were part of the first Big Push into the German lines at Loos where the initial charge was led by the 1/18th London Irish Rifles following a football booted into No Man's Land by Rifleman Frank Edwards. Shortly after, the overtly propagandist weekly, *The War Illustrated*, carried a dramatic full-page representation, not of Frank, but of a sporting young officer in an unnamed stretch of trench before 'a recent battle'. The caption further explained that this young sport had chalked the name of his regiment on the ball.

The remainder of the East Surreys joined their 1st battalion on the Somme in July 1916 where, highly reminiscent of Loos, a massive British bombardment was underway, designed to decimate enemy wire defences and remove the threat of their front line machine-gun posts. Leading the British charge was Captain Wilfred Percy ('Billie') Nevill of the 8th East Surreys. Almost certainly inspired by the illustration of the dashing young officer pictured in *War Illustrated* six months earlier, Nevill provided his men with the same reassuringly familiar rallying point in the form of a football for each of his platoons to be kicked ahead of the advance. Like the officer depicted in the popular magazine, Nevill chalked a message on each ball for the Hun. The Surreys were making for Montauban, the southern most of the Somme villages. Failure to reach it meant the difference between victory and defeat. Whereas the 47th Division at Loos reached all of its objectives, events conspired to undermine that success. While Edwards fell wounded and gassed, Nevill paid with his life on the blackest day in British military history. National heroes, the *Daily Mirror* showed men of the East Surreys cheering their comrades who had taken part in the advance. The fallen captain was pictured with Private Draper, 'one of the dribblers', holding a football, described as one of the 'sacred emblems of the battalion's heroism and devotion'. Sir Arthur Conan Doyle wrote of the battalion 'which, with the ineradicable sporting instinct and light-heartedness of the Londoner, had dribbled footballs, one for each platoon, across No Man's Land and shot their goal in the front-line trench.' An assiduous recorder of events on the Western Front, Conan Doyle failed to report the same sentiment expressed by those Londoners who had likewise led the way at Loos almost a year earlier.

Today, the Somme ranks reverentially with Ypres, Passendael and the other 'big' names evocative of the First World War, and rightly so. Loos, however, languishes as a failure in a passage of consummate catastrophes. Billie Nevill's footballing exploit was used by the propagandists to garner a measure of positivity. Loos followed the first Christmas of the conflict where fraternisation with the enemy followed that curiously companionable combination of sport and war. Strict orders were in place to prevent any repetition of this sporting rebellion. Then, as now, the language of conflict was ubiquitous in the words used to describe the etiquette of competitive sport with talk of battle and conquest, a clash of wills and the destruction of the opponent. Critics of sport's role in today's society often focus upon its competitive nature and claim that it can cause psychological scarring, similar to that of war. The more naive defenders of sport look to the playful nature of contest, where sporting competition is characterised by friendship rather than the enmity required for war, although in reality it is often difficult to differentiate between the warrior, the competitor and even the spectator at full tilt. Frank Edwards' footballing exploit was but one of a million individual acts of valour, heroism and audacity throughout the war to end all wars. His being there with his pals at the front, hatching a plan to confound the enemy with the unexpected, epitomises the character of hundreds of thousands across all classes, ranks and creeds, many who gave of their lives imbued with the necessary attributes of 'decency, fortitude, grit, civilisation, Christianity and commerce' all blended into a single virtue – 'The Game!'

Chapter One

Sport and War

Towards the end of the First World War, in 1918, when asked by Prime Minister David Lloyd George to paint a picture showing collaboration between British and US troops, John Singer Sargent rejected the commission and instead painted 'Gassed', his epic depiction of the aftermath of a mustard gas attack on the Western Front. In it, he includes a discreet but stark reminder of the close proximities of sport and war. In the distance, beyond the haunting lines of blinded soldiers painfully groping their way to a field dressing station, a football match is taking place. Some commentators suggest that the wounded ranks of soldiers are making their way towards eternal redemption, or that the eerie yellow glow of the polluted sky is in fact the sun setting on a society wasteful of its youth. But it is in the contrast between suffering and play that *Gassed* is also a comment on how sport is often used as a metaphor for war. When war broke out in 1914, many thousands of young men were inspired by the words of Sir Arthur Conan Doyle to fight for their country: 'If a cricketer had a straight eye, let him look along the barrel of a rifle ... if a footballer had strength of limb let them serve and march in the field of battle.'

Fewer men were refused military service in 1914 than were accepted. The nation as a whole was marginally better nourished than the previous generation where the factory and the mill financing Britain's greatness continued to take its toll. However, relatively few of those fighting for survival in the industrial stews of the towns and cities could boast a straight eye or strength of limb. The value of a proper diet was identified after the Crimean War but still remained an issue at the time of the Boer Wars. In Edwardian Britain, the lesson still needed to be learned that a healthier workforce not only meant increased productivity but also a fitter fighting force.

Frank Edwards was born on 29 September 1893 to Alfred, a coachman and Emily Jane, a domestic servant, who were living just off the King's Road, Chelsea.

In the 1960s this was the trendiest address in the world, but half a century earlier it was only marginally superior to the many decaying working class streets in the immediate area. The poverty and depredation, however, was relative to the upper middle class areas around Sloane Street, although much less onerous than the slums of London's East End. About a quarter of Chelsea's population was considered to be living in poverty when Frank, aged fourteen, was granted a requisition certificate from the Superintendent Registrar of Births and Deaths to enable him to quit school and begin full-time employment. The family had by this time moved out of the social housing provided by the Guinness Trust and were living at number 8 King Street, not far from the Stamford Bridge Athletics ground, acquired by Chelsea Football Club in 1905 when it was formed and entered the Football League. Fulham – the oldest of London's first class football clubs with a history stretching back to 1879 – had settled at Craven Cottage in 1896. As Frank grew up, so the game of football became a part of his life. Nearby Chelsea Barracks represented an even earlier connection with football history when the British Army was called upon to break up an unruly village game between the Derbyshire parishes of All Saint's and St Peters on Shrovetide Tuesday in 1846.

By the turn of the twentieth century, the growing popularity of and accessibility to sport went hand in hand with the radical concept of recreation. Participatory sport for the working classes was found principally in the form of association football, or soccer, and to a greater extent in the north of England, rugby. In the spring of 1914, King George V watched Burnley beat Liverpool in the FA Cup Final in front of 72,778 spectators. With the outbreak of war a few months later, men from the upper classes were 'allowed' to join regiments such as the First Sportsman's Battalion, the 23rd Royal Fusiliers. Gentlemen viewed sport as a pastime undertaken according to gentlemanly conduct with strict adherence to rules and fair play. It was not about winning, it was about taking part. In times of war, gentlemen became officers. To Britain's elite, the Battle of Waterloo was won on the playing fields of Eton. War was simply an extension of sport played at home, as the lyrics of the popular 1914 song 'Your King and Country' make plain:

> We've watched you playing cricket and every kind of game.
> At football, golf and polo you men have made your name.
> But now your country calls you to play your part in war.
> And no matter what befalls you we shall love you all the more.

Sir Henry Newbolt's '*Vitai Lampada*' was a popular poem that had for some time prior to the global conflict peddled the same union of sport and war:

> The River of death has brimmed its banks,
> And England's far, and Honour a name,

But the voice of a schoolboy rallies the ranks:
'Play up! Play up! And play the game.'

Endurance, submission to discipline, good temper, judgment, quickness of observation and self-control were all qualities deemed essential in a good polo player as in a good soldier. Lower down the social scale, however, it was football that was used during the first months of the First World War as a major incentive to enlistment, offering the chance to participate in what was described as 'The Greatest Game of all'.

Sport as a symbol for war and peace continues to motivate subsequent generations, but participation has never been enough. Losing is not an option. The heaviest member of India's first ever rugby team, Minal Pastala, maintained that 'competitive sport is like a war'. The eccentric American Media mogul, owner of the Atlanta Braves, evoker of the Goodwill Games and winner of the coveted America's Cup, Ted Turner, famously echoed George Orwell in stating that 'sport is like a war without the killing'. And Vietnam veteran, Michael Clancy, captured the irony well when he wrote in a song: 'there'll never be a sport quite like war'.

Sport has kept prisoners of war alive during the most appalling states of depravation, or has focused the mind on freedom. During the Second World War the Red Cross despatched footballs, rugby balls, cricket and tennis equipment and boxing gloves to captured troops. Otherwise, prisoners made do with what was at hand. British prisoners held at Stalag Luft III in Germany made golf balls from string and later more sophisticated versions manufactured from rubber gym shoes stitched in leather. They even built a golf course with 18 holes of 50–70 yards. The same camp gave rise to the classic prisoner of war film, *The Wooden Horse* where vaulting provided the screen for Allied soldiers' escape attempts.

In 1971 table tennis led to a discussion that resulted in a thawing of the relationship between the United States and China. What became known as 'ping-pong diplomacy' paved the way for President Nixon's breakthrough visit to China. 'It's fascinating what sport can do' recalled former US Secretary of State, Colin Powell, prior to a high-drama cricket series between India and Pakistan, which, he believed, would end decades of hostility. He pointed out that when people come together and travelled to each other's countries to watch a conflict played out on the field of sport, they better appreciate their differences. At the outbreak of the First World War some of Britain's leading sportsmen were among the first to join up. And of all the tennis and rugby players, rowers, athletes and cricketers, it was football that provided the bulk of professional sporting volunteers.

By the close of 1914 it is estimated that half-a-million men had joined up at football matches. By the following spring, all spectator sport throughout the

1. Navy internees playing football in Holland.

2. Indian Football Cup taking place in a British prisoners' camp in Germany.

British Isles, including professional football, had been banned. The book *Abide With Me* – written in 2003 by Frances David – celebrates the 89th anniversary of the Glossop North End players volunteering for duty at the local community hall. Here, as elsewhere throughout the country, young footballers especially were targeted because they were the most fit and disciplined of the Nation's youth. Through the memory, documents and letters of one widow, *Abide With Me* centres on the Derbyshire players who came to volunteer as part of a football battalion and how they ultimately sacrificed their young lives.

The most famous football battalion was the 17th (Service) Battalion (1st Football), or the Duke of Cambridge Own (Middlesex) Regiment, raised at the Richmond Athletic Ground on 12 December 1914 by the Right Honourable William Joynson Hicks, Member of Parliament for Brentford. Like the Artists', the Civil Service and other 'branded' rifle battalions raised primarily from a specific profession or group, the 17th Middlesex was comprised mostly of football players. In November 1915, it embarked for France where it was transferred to 6th brigade 2nd Division under the command of Frank Buckley, the first professional football manager of the modern school, appointed by Leeds. As a player, Buckley was a tough centre half, turning out for Aston Villa, Brighton, Manchester United, Manchester City, Birmingham, Derby County and Bradford City, and winning a cap for England against Ireland just before the outbreak of war. Having fought in the Boer War, he acquired the rank of major with The Footballers' Battalion and was wounded in the shoulder and lung in 1916. 'The Major', as he became known, recovered to become manager of Wolverhampton Wanderers.

While the 17th and its companion battalion, the 23rd (Service) attracted many London players, the 16th Royal Scots was doing the same north of the border. Author Jack Alexander meticulously lays out their story in his book, *McCrae's Battalion*, which was formed by Sir George McCrae in response to the call for sportsmen throughout the land to exchange the field of play for that of battle. For those who did not, the third Earl of Durham informed a patriotic meeting held on 11 November 1914 that he 'almost wished that the Germans would drop a shell among these footballers some Saturday afternoon' as the best method of 'waking up the young men'. Weeks later and every member of Heart of Midlothian – Scotland's most successful team – enlisted for the new Edinburgh battalion, inspiring many other footballers and fans to do likewise. The Edinburgh *Evening News* was moved to rebuke Celtic's win over Hearts for the championship in so far as it and Rangers had yet to send 'a single prominent player to the Army'. There was only one football champion in Scotland, it concluded, 'and its colours are maroon and khaki'. Seven members of the Hearts team never returned home. Three of them, Harry Wattie, Duncan Currie and Ernie Ellis, were killed on the first day of the Somme offensive.

3. The Sportsman's Battalion marching to camp in October 1914.

4. A football party on Belgium beach by James Thriar.

McCrae's Battalion, which included athletes from all sports, created a belief that the Germans would be ill-matched against such a physically well-honed and disciplined force. *The Greater Game*, a recent publication by respected battlefield guides Clive Harris and Julian Whippy, looks at a great number of sporting icons who fell in the First World War, across all the major sports including rugby union and rugby league, ice hockey, rowing, cricket and predominantly football. This focus on the beautiful game has drawn mild criticism from at least one reviewer, but then some sociologists and historians believe that football has become so popular because it requires abilities such as aim, speed, agility and tactics synonymous with warfare.

In both World Wars footballs made their way to British regiments as an important means of maintaining the fitness of troops and keeping up their morale. In the First World War it is said that no British troops ever travelled without footballs or the energy to kick them. One newspaper campaign saw thousands of footballs despatched to troops in France.

As the public schools and universities transformed a chaotic rural pastime, so a significant number of the officer class acquired a taste for the game.

5. Footballs as gifts.

Those of The Royal Engineers won the FA Cup in 1875 and were losing finalists on three occasions. Otherwise, football was predominantly the preserve of enlisted men. As well as a core element in the British Army's physical training programme, the biggest influence on the growth of the game was overseas in the days of empire. In the 1890s, regimental clubs in the Far East began to play against clubs in Singapore and Hong Kong. In Africa, army teams played in the first organised competitions in Cairo and in the Ethiopian capital Addis Ababa. The British Army was also instrumental in taking football to South Africa during the Boer Wars when it relied heavily on native baggage carriers. Games of football began to be played between the natives and soldiers and so the sport took off. In India a football tournament between regiments stationed in Calcutta led to the Duran Cup, the third oldest football tournament in the world, first won by the Royal Scots Fusiliers in 1888. Local clubs were formed and were soon claiming famous victories. As one newspaper reported: 'It fills every Indian's heart with joy and pride to know that rice-eating, malaria-ridden barefooted Bengalis have got the better of beef-eating Herculean, booted John Bull in the peculiarly English sport.' A remnant of Britain's colonial past survives (at the time of writing) as The Kop at Anfield, named in memory of the many Liverpool lads serving in the British army who died in the fierce battle fought in January 1900 against the Boers at Spion Kop, or Spy Hill.

In his beautifully illustrated book, *War Game*, children's writer Michael Foreman tells the story of four friends that were in reality his uncles Will, Lacey, Billy and Freddie, all of whom were killed in the First World War. Foreman's moving account begins in the summer of 1914 with the four lads playing football near their home in Suffolk and ends at Christmas time with 'an energetic match, played across the wastes of No Man's Land, with no rules or referee, and greatcoats and caps for goals'. A few days later and 'the friendly Germans from Saxony' were replaced by less favoured troops from Prussia. Countering their attack, the British Tommies scramble over the top and in a dramatic conclusion, Freddie, who still has the football, boots it towards the enemy. The others follow, as one by one they are all tackled and eventually cut down by machine-gun fire. As *War Game* encompasses the complete spectrum of footballing bravado peculiar to the First World War, so it reinforces a mythology that blends fact with fiction.

In *Great War and Modern Memory*, Paul Fussell surveys First World War poetry, drama, fiction, memoirs, letters and general culture, 'finding in them earlier influences, and also tracing their influence on subsequent twentieth-century writing, culture, and thought'. In this he explains 'one way of showing the sporting spirit was to kick a football toward the enemy lines while attacking' and is the only historian to credit the 1st Battalion/18th London Regiment at

The War Illustrated, 13th February, 1915.   Page 530.

Footballers to Play the Greater Game

Members of the Footballers' Battalion training hard in the grounds of the White City for their forthcoming match with the Huns. On account of their sport, they are already men of the finest physique.

Doubling after the trainer in the Exhibition grounds—a form of exercise at which the footballers should be fairly adept.

More members of the Footballers' Battalion at drill at the erstwhile pleasure resort, Shepherd's Bush.

Footballers as professional soldiers. Prominent players attend at the headquarters of their battalion to receive Army pay. By the table on the right are Mr. F. J. Wall, Secretary of the Football Association, Colonel Grantham, and Captain Elphinstone.

6. The Footballer's Battalion training at White City, West London.

7. War Game. (Reproduced by kind permission of Michael Foreman)

Loos in 1915 as the first to show this spirit. 'Soon,' he adds, 'it achieved the status of a conventional act of bravado' which was ultimately exported far beyond the Western Front. At Beersheba in Turkey in November 1917 Arthur ('Bosky') Burton took part in an attack on the Turkish lines and proudly reported home: 'one of the men had a football. How it came there goodness knows. Anyway we kicked off and rushed the first [Turkish] guns, dribbling the ball with us.'

Chapter Two

Footballs at Dawn

That sport and war are inextricably linked as a potent mixture of adversarial posturing is all too evident to this day when an England versus Germany football match is bound by official warnings not to mention 'the war'. What enmity exists is predominantly expressed by English fans and refined to a mostly comedic cocktail of terrace banter agitating late twentieth-century political correctness. Before 1938 an England versus Germany football match carried none of the baggage that it does today. Although a minor episode in the greater scheme of things, football was hugely important to men of both sides and across all ranks in the First World War. Days before the famous Christmas Truce of 1914, Major John Charteris, Staff Officer to General Haig, having nothing much to do, 'turned out to play football for the staff against a team of cavalry' which included the Prince of Wales. The amount of newspaper coverage afforded the famous Truce was because it happened over such a wide area and extended period of time. It immediately captured the popular imagination, carrying as far as Australia and the United States. What principally kept it alive were the number of letters sent to the newspapers rather than editorial comment. The principal reaction was one of amazement. On 1 January 1915 the *South Wales Echo* reported:

> When the history of the war is written one of the episodes which chroniclers will seize upon as one of its most surprising features will undoubtedly be the manner in which the foes celebrated Christmas. How they fraternized in each other's trenches, played football, rode races, held sing songs, and surprisingly adhered to their unofficial truce will certainly go down as one the greatest surprises of a surprising war.

The Christmas Truce has been described as an agreeable interference and a sentimental aside in the dialogue of war. But there was a more serious undercurrent, a belief, albeit a naive one, that what the men themselves were doing would somehow bring the fighting to an end. An RAF Officer in the Second World War musing on the subject believed

> ... if only all the soldiers along the whole of the Western Front refused to go back to the slaughter, then millions of lives would have been saved. Hitler's rise to power might have been stymied and a Second World War averted.

The 1914 Christmas Truce has become the quintessential stage upon which football at the front is associated. It has inspired a jazz suite called *No Man's Land*, described as a poetic story of love and separation told partly through the songs of the time including a version of Silent Night. *Oh What a Lovely War* is a play originally produced at Joan Littlewood's Theatre Workshop in East London and later filmed by Sir Richard Attenborough. It includes the incident when the slaughtering ended temporarily to share food, exchange photographs and memories, and to play games of football. The same theme underlies Paul McCartney's video to his 1983 No.1 hit single *Pipes of Peace. The Truce* is a multi-award winning short film studying the relationship between enemy soldiers during a First World War Christmas Day ceasefire, and similarly *Merry Christmas*, the official entry for the 2004 Best Foreign Language Film Oscar, follows the fortunes of Scottish, French and German troops who decided to put their differences aside in the name of peace for one day.

8. Still from *The Truce*, directed by Eric Rolnick.

The naturalist, journalist, broadcaster and author of over fifty books, Henry Williamson, joined the 5th Battalion, The London Rifle Brigade, City of London Regiment, Territorial Forces, in January 1914. After the declaration of war, he was mobilised on 5 August that same year, marching out of London for training in Sussex. By November he was fighting in France and was an eyewitness to the fraternisation on Christmas Eve, which made a deep and lasting impression upon his life. His fifteen volume semi-autobiographical *A Chronicle of Ancient Sunlight* follows the life of Phillip Maddison and his family from the turn of the century until the 1950s, including Williamson's seminal experiences in the First World War in which he saw that war was created by greed, misplaced zeal and bigotry. He was profoundly moved to discover that German soldiers thought just as deeply and sincerely as did their English counterparts fighting for God and Country.

He determined through his writing to do what he could to prevent war and promote understanding. *A Fox Under My Cloak* (volume five of *A Chronicle of Ancient Sunlight*) devotes sixteen of its 200 pages to Williamson's fictional account of Phillip Maddison's experiences of the Christmas Truce. Chapter Three, *'Heilige Nacht'*, sees Phillip Maddison and his platoon tasked with making twin wire fences in place of a flooded communications trench when he sees a strange light on top of a pole put up in the German lines, followed by a cheer from the occupants of 'Hoch! Hoch! Hoch!' Crouching and ready to fling himself flat, the expected barrage does not occur. Instead there are the cheers wafting across No Man's Land accompanying the dim outline of figures on the German parapet. Then to his amazement and that of his platoon, he sees lights set upon a Christmas tree with the enemy huddled around it talking, laughing and cheering 'Hoch! Hoch! Hoch!' Mr Thoverton, the platoon commander, looks at his watch and confirms that it is eleven o'clock. By Berlin time, it was midnight. 'A merry Christmas to everyone!' he declares, as from the German parapet wafts a rich baritone voice singing a song Phillip remembered his nurse singing to him, *Stille Nache*.

Unofficial truces are by no means rare events. Food was shared and stories exchanged between Union and Confederate troops during the American Civil War, and British soldiers consorted with the French during the Peninsular War, with the Russians in the Crimea and with the Boers in South Africa. The approach of Christmas 1914 saw similar spontaneous exchanges set against what was widely perceived as a truly senseless war. The relatively modest British Army manning the Western Front at that time held a stretch of the line running south from the Ypres salient for 27 miles to the La Bassée Canal. The enemy was often as close as 30 yards away and so incidents of fraternisation between both factions were not uncommon. As Christmas approached, so the very real desire for a lull in the fighting increased with festive cards and parcels from home. The British troops

9. Henry Williamson.
(Henry Williamson
Literary Estate)

received plum puddings, 'Princess Mary boxes' filled with chocolates, butter-scotch, cigarettes and tobacco. German troops received large meerschaum pipes and boxes of cigars for the officers. Belgian and French troops also received gifts, but with their countries occupied, they largely failed to share the same appetite for consorting with the enemy as their British allies. Many accounts of the 1914 Christmas Truce, some written long after the event, are confused or contradic-tory. The common denominator, however, is invariably the playing of football.

On Christmas Day, Henry Williamson's Phillip Maddison makes the most of the unusual peace to take a bike ride and have lunch in a local village. A passing solider tells him that everyone was in No Man's Land. Walking into the crowd, he finds himself face to face with the enemy exchanging addresses, souvenirs, food, chatting away and burying their dead. He is told they are Saxons who had watched him and his pals put up the fence on Christmas Eve, but they did not fire and would not have done and even if they were ordered to they would have fired high. 'Not a bad lot o' bleders, if you arst me, mate,' one Tommy observes before another surprise, when a football is kicked into the air, and several men run after it. 'The upshot was a match proposed between the two armies, to be held in a field behind the German lines.'

In a history of the 1st Battalion, Royal Irish Rifles, the Commanding Officer, Lieutenant-Colonel George Laurie, claims that it was he who crossed to the

German trenches on Christmas Day, armed only with a three-day-old copy of the *Daily Telegraph*. Eventually others joined him and the two sides exchanged gifts, admired family photographs and talked. Laurie makes no mention of a football match being played on his sector of the front. *The Times* for 1 January 1915, confirms that the 6th Gordon Highlanders organised a burial truce with the enemy before the fraternisation began, which included impromptu games of football. A major in the Medical Corps reported that the Germans beat the British 3–2. Kurt Zehmisch of the 134th Saxons recorded in his diary:

> The English brought a soccer ball from the trenches, and pretty soon a lively game ensued. How marvellously wonderful, yet how strange it was. The English officers felt the same way about it. Thus Christmas, the celebration of Love, managed to bring mortal enemies together as friends for a time.

In exchange for a tin of bully beef, Lieutenant Ian Stewart was given a photograph of the German pre-war football team.

> I could talk some German, and one of the German officers; some English … Our conversation was no different from that of meeting a friendly opponent at a football match.

One former soldier reminiscing in the 1920s confirmed that 'footer' was an inevitable part of the occasion, sometimes using a tin can or a rolled-up sandbag

10. Pictorial proof of the Christmas Day Truce.

as well as a genuine leather ball. One German lieutenant wrote: 'We marked the goals with our caps. Teams were quickly established for a match on the frozen mud, and the Fritz's beat the Tommies 3–2.' Like Captain Hulse, not all of those in charge of discipline approved. One officer ordered to prepare a more usable pitch by filling in shell holes refused to comply and so the proposed match did not take place. Some local Frenchwomen were also deeply unimpressed and spat at members of one British battalion the next time they were in town. Another former infantrymen writing of the Christmas Truce in the 1920s recalled that the men who joined them later

> … were inclined to disbelieve us when we spoke of the incident, and no wonder, for as the months rolled by, we who were actually there could hardly realise that it had happened, except for the fact that every little detail stood out well in our memory.

The Christmas Truce has subsequently captured the popular imagination to become the iconic footballing passage of The Great War. But the first recorded football kicked in anger towards the enemy lines was that at Loos nine months later. On Christmas 1914, the man who would kick it was halfway through his training with the London Irish Rifles in Hertfordshire, learning how to kill and to survive, as well as conquering all on the football pitch. Frank Edwards and his pals would have read about the Truce and probably have better appreciated the connection with sport and war than the subtleties of front line politics. Maybe they hoped, as did many others, that this was a precursor of an early settlement, that the leaders on both sides would see the same sense as the men on the ground. For any football-mad young man the idea of playing the game on No Man's Land after months of fighting would have stood out as the single most positive episode to take with him on his journey to the trenches. Come the day, Edwards would keep a deflated ball tucked into his tunic at all times, ready to be inflated and put into action at any given opportunity. And none better than the start of first Great Push of the war when his regiment would be chosen to lead the assault. Ignoring official warnings, he would save his ball from the pistol shots puncturing others once his plan was known.

Frank's moment and that of his footballing pals was to be as brief as the meagre amount of interest afforded the action of the 47th Division at Loos, and indeed the battle itself. The 1st Battalion London Irish Rifles was mentioned in despatches as the regiment that had saved an entire Army Corps; they had met their objectives after four days resisting counter attacks until at last they were relieved. It would later be revealed that had the reserves passed through the captured lines within an hour as planned, then the success at Loos would have been consolidated, the enemy possibly routed and perhaps the war shortened by many months. The repercussions were to be serious. Allied to this perceived failure was the decision for the British to use chlorine gas for the first time at Loos. According to *The War Illustrated* – that significant constituent of the government propaganda machine – the employment of asphyxiating gases had preoccupied public attention since its first use by the enemy in the spring of 1915.

Lachrymatory gas shells (tear gas) were used by the Allies as far back as 1914, but it was the Germans who first used chlorine, to deadly effect. Prior to the first Great Push at Loos, *The War Illustrated* addressed what it declared to be the confusion in the public mind between the savage inhumanity of the Hun and Britain's more enlightened approach to the use of poison gas. This bewilderment was explained in the manner in which the Germans broke the conventions of 'civilised' warfare while not infringing any convention in their employment of poison gas. Its use had in fact been supported by Britain and America at the Hague Convention in 1907 and opposed by Germany. But where the latter had agreed not to use the weapon against the armies of other absenting nations, its use would be legitimised against troops fighting alongside those who supported its use, such as the British. Whereas Britain was not against the use of asphyxiating shells, it did condemn unequivocally the 'savage nature' of the methods employed by an enemy that decided to use 'scientific torture', resulting in a long and agonising death.

Long before the Germans resorted to the use of its 'torture gas', *The War Illustrated* revealed that they had for years been engineering a subtle and deadly form of poison attack on an unprecedented scale. Shells had been found in captured German munitions stores that were designed to carry toxic chemicals into wounded bodies. Sparing no detail in explaining the tragic after-effects of phosphorus poisoning, the paper was content to let the matter rest, calling upon 'everybody in the British Empire' not to allow such things to continue without seriously considering the legitimate use of asphyxiating gas. The consequences of doing nothing may result in 'many long, terrible, years in a war of extermination', readers were advised. Meanwhile, Allied soldiers were gaily depicted in their respirators and anti-gas masks, as quite the fashion in the trenches. 'Even Poisonous Gas has its Humorous Side' announced one cheery headline to 'an amusing scene' of French bandsmen attempting to play their instruments under threat of a German gas attack. 'Not an Egyptian mummy' jibed another skittish observation, but a Scottish soldier wearing a robust respirator.

Had the reserves arrived on time at Loos then the day would have been won, the use of chlorine gas justified and perhaps the attack of the 47th Division following a football the stuff of popular appeal. Frank Edwards may have been feted as a hero and his story enshrined in the historical record. As it happened, it was to be the events on the first day of the Somme that grabbed the attention. On 1 July 1916, the 7th Buffs occupied the foremost section of trench

11. Fixing 'respirators', August 1915.

closest to the German line. The 8th Norfolks were positioned to the left of them, with the 7th Queens to the right. To their right and chosen to lead the charge was the 8th East Surreys commanded by Captain Wilfred Percy ('Billie') Nevill. Nine months earlier, in the autumn of 1915, the 7th and 8th Battalions, East Surreys, had fought at Loos. Now the remainder joined their 1st Battalion where a similar massive British artillery bombardment was underway, failing to destroy the enemy wire defences and front line machine-gun posts. Writing to his wife Else on 28 June, Nevill described 'the shells are fairly haring over; you know one gets just sort of bemused after a few million, still it'll be a great experience to tell one's children about'.

The London Irish had been making for the village of Loos, the Surreys for Montauban, the southern most of the Somme villages. Failure to reach it meant the difference between victory and defeat. Just as Rifleman Edwards had contrived for the charge, so Captain Nevill provided his men with the same reassuringly familiar rallying point. At home it would epitomise grit, determination and raw courage, but would in Germany be viewed as a clear example of British madness. Nevill undoubtedly seized on the heroic image of the footballer published in the October 1915 edition of *The War Illustrated*. This was 'an episode which strikingly illustrates the proverbial sporting spirits of Britons on the battlefield', the caption explained. This 'recent assault' on the German trenches began despite the din of exploding artillery shells about their ears, with 'the whispered order' to charge. Then, with 'lightening rapidity' as every man stormed over the parapet, the officer kicked off the football with his platoon members names chalked on it. 'Follow up, lads!' he shouted, leading the way, only to be struck down before he had covered a few paces.

What Frank Edwards and his fellow footballers made of this parody can only be imagined. There was no question of dropping a letter of complaint to the editor of *The War Illustrated*. The baton had been passed to the right sort. Such an image would have appealed to keen young leaders such as Billie Nevill who would have appreciated the audacity and, by the summer of 1916, the value beyond the heroic image in providing a more affirmative focus for their men other than the sight and sound of shot and shell scything through the ranks. So it was that when on leave back home Nevill purchased two – some accounts say four – footballs, one for each of his platoons to be kicked ahead of the advance. The platoon that penetrated furthest into German territory would win a prize. Instead of chalking the names of the members of his platoon on the ball, as *The War Illustrated* had contrived, Nevill had painted onto one: 'The Great European Cup. The Final. East Surreys v Bavarians. Kick off at Zero' and on another 'No Referee'.

The Battle of Loos started on 25 September 1915 and ended three weeks later on 16 October. In total, 61,000 British officers and other ranks were killed or

12. 'Gallant Officer scores a Goal on the Field of War'.

injured against the German losses of less than 20,000. In contrast, by nightfall of the first day on the Somme, there were 57,470 casualties out of the 120,000 men who had left the trenches that morning. Some 21,000 men had been killed in the first 30 minutes of the attack. No fewer than twelve divisions suffered over 3,000 casualties each. The 1st Hampshires and the 10th West Yorks were decimated in under a minute. The same assurance issued as that prior to the charge at Loos was equally flawed. The barbed wire and machine-guns were not destroyed by the enormous artillery bombardment. Instead the attackers found themselves caught in the open and cut down.

The night before the start of the Somme offensive, Captain Nevill had supervised the removal of the barbed wire in front of the British trenches, issued ammunition, sandbags, flares, tools and sufficient food to last each man 48 hours. At 04.30 hours he ate his breakfast and downed his ration of rum. At 06.30 on 1 July 1916, he watched the mist lift off the flat terrain. At 07.27, fourteen days off his 22nd birthday, he led his men into No Man's Land. One account has him down as 'the battalion buffoon', although he was shrewder than that, knowing full well that the attack was not going to be the walkover widely believed. Another account suggests that he was inspired by Henry Newbolt's poem *Vitai Lampada* about the cricketing hero 'playing the game'. This is echoed in another verse written by the *Daily Mail's* 'Touchstone', scribbled on the border of an undated field concert program held at the Imperial War Museum. Headed: 'A Company of the East Surrey Regiment is reported to have dribbled four footballs – the gift of their Captain – who fell in the fight & dash for a mile and a quarter into the enemy trenches', the celebration is entitled 'The Game':

> On through the hail of slaughter,
> Where gallant comrades Fall,
> Where blood is poured like water,
> They drive the trickling ball.
> The fear of death before them
> Is but an empty name.
> True to the land that bore them –
> The SURREYS play the game.

A survivor recalling zero hour tells of how when the gun-fire died away he saw an infantryman climb onto the parapet into No Man's Land, beckoning others to follow.

> Subject to the proviso that proper formation and distance was not lost thereby, he kicked off a football. A good kick. The ball rose and travelled well towards the German line. That seemed to be the signal to advance.

No sooner were the 'players' making their run than it became apparent that the dugouts sheltering the German troops had proved too effective. As the bombardment ceased, signalling the imminent attack, so they were able to set up their machine-guns to cut down the British as they left the relative safety of their trenches.

One of Nevill's fellow officers later wrote to his family: 'the company went over the top very well, with your brother kicking off the company footballs.' Sir Arthur Conan Doyle reported in his history of *The British Campaign in France and Flanders, 1916*:

> No sooner had the troops come out from cover than they were met by a staggering fire which held them up in the Breslau Trench. The supports had soon to be pushed up to thicken the ranks of the East Surreys – a battalion which, with the ineradicable sporting instinct and light-heartedness of the Londoner, had dribbled footballs, one for each platoon across No Man's Land and shot their goal in the front-line trench.

13. The Surreys play the game.

14. A sacred emblem of the East Surreys' heroism.

15. Private Draper, one of the East Surreys' 'dribblers'.

Fierce fighting raged for some time around a crater formed by a mine explosion. An officer and a sergeant of the Buffs killed twelve Germans and cut off their flow of reinforcements, while half a company of the same battalion cleared the crater and captured a machine-gun post. The brigade was making headway against hard German resistance. Captain Nevill had dashed to the front, reformed his own men and led them onwards. By 07.50 hours the Battalion had raced the mile-and-a-half to the German front line. Seven of the 8th East Surreys' officers were killed in the attack, including Nevill's second in command, Lieutenant R. E. Soames, who had kicked off the second football. Billie Nevill himself lay dead just outside the German wire. Two of the footballs were later recovered after 'the goal was won' and taken back to the regimental depot at Kingston.

The *Daily Mirror* published a picture of Lieutenant Colonel H. P. Treeby DSO standing alongside one of the footballs leading the cheers for the men who took part in the advance. Together with a portrait of Captain Nevill, the accompanying report told of how he

> ... fell during the attack on Montauban, kicked off this football, which the 8th East Surreys dribbled under withering fire right into the German trenches. This sacred emblem of the battalion's heroism and devotion has just arrived at the regimental depot, when stirring scenes occurred. On the day in question the Surreys fought the Prussian Guard.

Also pictured was Private Draper, described as 'one of the dribblers'.

William Beach Thomas, the *Daily Mail's* notoriously fatuous war correspondent, wrote of Nevill's attack:

> On they came kicking footballs, and so completely puzzled the Potsdammers. With one last kick they were amongst them with the bayonet, and although the Berliners battled bravely for a while, they kameraded with the best.

The British press took up the story as a measure of optimism plucked from a mire of unmitigated disaster. Captain Billie Nevill became a national hero. A decade would pass before Frank Edwards' footballing inspiration gained, albeit limited, recognition.

Chapter Three

Frank Edwards, Volunteer

In his autobiographical account, *The Great Push*, documenting his experiences as a stretcher-bearer with the London Irish Rifles, the Irish writer and self-proclaimed 'Navvy poet', Patrick MacGill recalls a boy coming along the trench at about 04.00am on the day of the attack at Loos carrying a football under his arm. 'Where are you going with that?' MacGill asked the lad. 'It's some idea, this,' laughed the boy, 'we're going to kick it across into the German trench.' MacGill agreed that it was some idea, going on to ask what were the chances of victory in such a game. 'The playing will tell' the boy answered. If that boy was Frank Edwards, fresh-faced and cheeky and with his plan all worked out, then MacGill's perception was spot on, for that same open face masked a tragedy that would haunt the man for the rest of his life.

On 8 February 1913 Frank Edwards married Georgina Evans. He was then aged nineteen and working as a stationer's assistant in the City of London. Georgina, a year younger, had recently been working at the Census Office. Frank lived at 8 King Street, Chelsea, and Georgina in the nearby Guinness Trust Buildings with her father, Henry, a newsagent. Both being under the age of 21, Frank and Georgina required the consent of their parents to marry, suggesting the obvious reason for the union.

Illegitimacy had traditionally been stigmatised in English society with unwed mothers and their infants seen as an affront to morality. Even family could not always be depended upon to offer comfort and aid. If a young unmarried woman became pregnant, her family as well as friends and employer often scorned her. It was not unusual for a girl 'in trouble' to be forced to leave her neighbourhood in disgrace and to go to an area where she was not known. The Bastardy Laws were amended in 1872 to make the acknowledged father equally liable for the support of the illegitimate child until the age of sixteen, but marriage, often hurriedly arranged, was the preferred option. So it was with

Frank and Georgina. From the rooms they rented in Sydney Street, a few minutes walk from the King's Road and Knightsbridge, Frank would travel each day to work in Leadenhall Market in the City of London.

At the time of Georgina's pregnancy serious infections such as puerperal sepsis killed mothers after childbirth. General Practice at that time covered male workers but not their wives and families, who were required to pay a fee. Therefore, half the babies born were delivered at home, either by a midwife or a woman experienced in childbirth. Pain relief in labour was rarely, if ever, provided in the home. Pre-eclampsia develops in the second half of pregnancy, usually in the last few weeks. Sometimes it starts as late as during labour or even just after the baby is born. When it became clear that things were going wrong with Georgina's pregnancy, Frank would have summoned a GP who might or might not have had the necessary skills. In some areas there were obstetric 'flying squads' attached the local hospital to deal with haemorrhage, shock and eclampsia. In Chelsea there was the Infirmary where Georgina was taken and where Frank witnessed her painful death and that of their child. Whether or not he drank to the extent he did in later life we do not know. Perhaps it was the agonising manner of Georgina's death that triggered his addiction. Possibly that look in his eye captured by Patrick MacGill was one of a pain half disguised by sham levity and a penchant for devilment and daring-do. Maybe he genuinely wondered what else life had to throw at him.

A year later, on Sunday 2 August 1914, the London Irish Rifles Territorial Army unit had arrived for its summer camp at Perham Down, but within an hour after 'Lights Out' the men were roused with orders to return at once to Headquarters in London for embodiment, to support the regular army. Two days later and with the nation at war with Germany, serving professionals in the British Army made up the four divisions of the British Expeditionary Force bound immediately for France. If deemed fit, retired regulars placed on Reserve also found themselves on French soil sooner rather than later. The Territorials were called upon to serve overseas and an appeal went out from Field-Marshal Lord Kitchener for 100,000 volunteers to swell their ranks. Until they were closed down for the duration, football grounds, race courses and other sporting venues put on displays of national unity enhanced with rousing music played by military bands and stirring speakers urging young men to join 'the team' and play 'the greatest game of all.' Footballers especially were encouraged to sign up in front of stands and terraces packed with admiring spectators. The Football Association claimed that its campaign alone produced over half-a-million volunteers, and such was the response that the required medical and health standards for the new recruits were temporarily increased to stem the sheer weight of numbers rapidly overwhelming the Regular Army's limited facilities.

Your King and Country Need You!

A CALL TO ARMS!

An addition of 100,000 men to His Majesty's Regular Army is immediately necessary in the present grave National Emergency. Lord Kitchener is confident that this appeal will be at once responded to by all those who have the safety of our Empire at heart.

TERMS OF SERVICE:
General Service for a period of 3 years or until the War is concluded.
Age of Enlistment between 19 and 30.

HOW TO JOIN.
Full information can be obtained at any Post Office in the United Kingdom or at any Military Depot.

God Save the King.

16. Newspaper recruitment notice, August 1914.

17. A London recruiting office, August 1914.

18. London Irish Rifles
recruitment poster.

On 7 August Frank Edwards took himself along to the Duke of York's Headquarters to sign up with the London Irish Rifles. Not that he was Irish or had any connection with Ireland. Volunteers had a considerable choice over which regiment they joined and many travelled long distances to attend a depot or recruiting office for a particular unit. Possibly they would be attracted to a regiment or corps by its reputation, but more often than not they opted for their local unit to be with their relatives or pals. As one of the initial 100,000 men 'of a particularly good type', Edwards, a keen and proficient sportsman, easily met the criteria. An exacting medical examination classified him into a service grade for overseas duty that declared him to be fit and able and free of any serious organic diseases, and with sound sight and hearing. He gave his age as 23 years and eleven months, although he was just about to turn 23, probably for the same reason he chose not to declare himself a widower. He took the King's shilling from the recruiting sergeant and with his liking for beer perhaps spent the token toasting patriotism, adventure and the call to arms, the primary motivators for many a volunteer. Or maybe, like those who joined for other reasons, to escape the toil of the plough or the drudgery of the factory clock, or to prove something to themselves, Frank Edwards quietly determined to make fresh start or meet his end with a touch of glory.

★ ★ ★

The Territorial Army came about as a result of the reorganisation of the former militia and other volunteer units to create a force of non-professional soldiers organised primarily for the defence of the realm. The London Regiment comprised rifle units drawn from all walks of life across the vast expanse of the capital. These included battalions of Post Office employees and artists; west of Piccadilly was the London Irish and east of Aldgate the 17th Poplar and Stepney. With the City of London Rifles in between, the Blackheath and Woolwich lay south of the river. Because of the sheer numbers of recruits it was to able attract, The London Regiment fielded two complete divisions when the Territorial Force divisions were numbered in 1915.

In 1914, the 1st Battalion 18th (County of London) Regiment, Territorial Force, London Irish Rifles was part of the 5th London Brigade, 2nd London Division, created by the establishment of the Territorial Force in 1908. Their base in Chelsea is now part of a sophisticated £120m redevelopment representing one of the most significant urban regeneration schemes of recent times. The Duke of York's Headquarters itself began as part of the vast expanse of Georgian military development, which includes the Royal Hospital and the National Army Museum. Purchased by the government during the reign of King George III to house the Royal Military Asylum for the Children of Soldiers of the Regular Army, the last of the boy orphans left The Duke of York's HQ in 1909 when it was set up as a base for the Territorial Force. A presence was maintained there until the late 1990s when 600 volunteers comprising the reserve force in Chelsea, included one company of London Irish Rifles.

19. The Duke of York's Headquarters, Chelsea *c.*1900.

Frank Edwards and his fellow volunteers reported each day to the Duke of York's Headquarters. This being the first and the largest draft, and the parade ground capable of holding only around 500 men for squad drill, half the battalion exercised from 9am to 1pm and the other half from 2pm onwards. Hyde Park was used for the full battalion to train together before the move was made to the vast 1905 Franco-British Exhibition complex at White City. The stadium built there for the 1908 Olympics introduced the new recruits to individual and unit discipline, how to follow commands and basic field craft with serving officers and seasoned Territorials assisting in preparing the new intake for the real thing. Uniforms were supplied only from the waist down and supplemented with a lapel badge consisting of a London Irish button on a backing of green cloth. Whereas it had previously taken eleven months to turn out a trained soldier, that time was now reduced to seven.

Before 1914, Territorials were rarely sent overseas but almost as soon as war was declared invitations were sent out to accept 'Foreign Service Obligation'. Those who declined – and many did – were withdrawn and sent to a home service unit. Many later changed their minds and rejoined their comrades a few months before leaving for France. By the end of October 1914, half the infantry brigades, including the London Irish Rifles, had marched north from London to their war stations at Hatfield, Watford or St Albans to undergo thorough platoon and company training. Musketry training, where it was available, relied heavily on the old style Mark I Long Lee Enfield rifle, although for the most part the combatants were equipped with new, small-bore, bolt-action weapons capable of firing multiple rounds from a spring-loaded clip inserted into a magazine.

Rivalling only the German Mauser both in terms of use and reputation, the Short Magazine Lee-Enfield Mark III took its name from its American

20. London recruits for the New Army starting their first drill in Hyde Park.

designer, James Lee and its manufacturer, the Royal Small Arms Factory based in Enfield, London. With its ten-cartridge magazine, it allowed a trained soldier to fire off twelve well-aimed shots a minute. Tens of thousands of volunteers, however, including the men of the London Irish, would arrive in France and be sent into battle with weapons that were both obsolete and inaccurate. Although these vintage rifles were adjusted to take the new .303 ammunition they were limited to single shots. Lieutenant Colonel G. A. Brett of the 1st Battalion 23rd London Regiment, reflecting after the Battle of Loos, would write: 'it was found that everyone in the battalion had exchanged his long rifle for the new short weapon with which the regular and service battalions were armed.' Although the men would be praised for rearming themselves with the modern and more trustworthy weapon, they were unable to acquire the long bayonets. Requests for them made to Army Ordnance were met with incredulity in so far as Territorial units had the effrontery to equip themselves with that 'to which they were not entitled'. The battalion would then be required to hand back the new weapons in return for their old long rifles. The war would be fully into its second year before every British soldier had access to the latest weaponry.

Initially, the British Expeditionary Force and its French allies proved successful in achieving objectives at the Battles of Mons and the Marne. By September 1914, as both sides tried unsuccessfully to outflank each other, the huge trench system that would become synonymous with the war to end all wars was taking shape. What would become known as the Western Front represented a contested armed frontier between lands controlled by Germany to the east and the Allies to the west. It would comprise an intricate system of burrows and trenches running from the Belgium coast, through northern France to the German border for some 460 miles in length and up to 20 miles in width. Apart from air raids and sea-based attacks on German bases, all of the fighting that would take place in France and Belgium would be mainly confined to the regions of north and west France and Flanders. It would be in this highly fortified area lined with trenches and peppered with dugouts, pillboxes and concrete forts, that over the course of the next four years, millions of soldiers would experience hell on earth. Ypres, Passchendael, the Somme and Verdun would rank amongst the most poignant battle names fought against a background of disease, mud, vermin and squalor interspersed with periods of sustained shelling and fierce hand-to-hand fighting.

By October 1914, with a war of attrition already seeded, it is ironic to consider the new recruits undergoing training in Britain looking upon spells of trench digging as a welcome relief from the monotony of square bashing and endless drill. An especially wet winter, which created great delays in obtaining equipment, telephones, transport and even basic clothing, only hinted at the far greater and more lethal discomforts to come, although the billeting of so many men at such short notice did offer a flavour of the rough times ahead.

21. Learning the art of trench digging in a London park.

While most local householders close to the war camps provided a roof for as many volunteers as could be crammed into what spare space was available, every school, parish hall and public building was filled to capacity, with hundreds of less fortunate recruits crowded into leaking barns and other farm buildings. But by all accounts spirits remained high and for most volunteers the experience was a positive one. Frank Edwards was able to display his sporting prowess to great effect as captain of 'a very respectable' London Irish football team, winning the Brigade Final on 2 January 1915 by beating the 20th Battalion 3–2. With a 5–0 win over the 24th Battalion the following week, the Army Service Corps received a 7–0 thrashing on 23 February when brigade and divisional training was completed.

At 3am on 8 March 1915, roll call was taken in the village street before sun up. Frank's battalion assembled on the Common as best it could in the semi-darkness. Once all the men were in position, twelve from each platoon marched up to Battalion Headquarters to fetch six heavy boxes, which were set down on the grass and opened up. From each were taken 20 khaki-coloured cotton bandoliers containing cartridges, 125 rounds of which were issued to the 50 men in each platoon and packed into their ammunition pouches. While adding a further eight unwelcome pounds in weight to an already punishing personal consignment, the ammunition signalled a welcome end to training and the beginning of the real thing.

As trained soldiers, the men had learned the difference between life in civvie street and the discipline of a khaki uniform. In the army there were only orders.

Fairness never entered into it. To complain was to flirt with insubordination. It was entirely counter-productive and could result in imprisonment for days or even years. It followed that orders were to be obeyed without hesitation. Even the act of walking was now a brisk, crisp affair instead of ambling along. Boots had to be spotless, buttons fastened, clothes brushed and cap worn straight over a shaven head. Half a year's solid training and Frank Edwards could shoot a rifle, plunge a bayonet (into a sack), throw a bomb, dig a trench and build a wire entanglement. He had an idea what it was like to march under shellfire and to advance in open order against a wall of enemy machine-gun fire. Day after day rehearsals included advancing and retiring, attacking and counter attacking, with little or no real comprehension of the appalling reality to come.

For the first time since signing up, Edwards could now make out an order (in triplicate) to the Quartermaster for spare boots, as many socks, shirts and other essentials as he was able to carry. He was issued with an enamelled bottle capable of holding one quart of water and a mess-tin, which could be used either as a saucepan or a cup, with the lid serving as a frying pan or a plate. 'Small kit' included a pocket knife with integral tin opener, tableware in the form of a knife, fork and spoon, razors, washing gear, spare bootlaces and something called a 'housewife' for mending torn clothing. Other extras included boracic powder to sooth blistered feet, a money belt, a luminous wristwatch and khaki handkerchiefs instead of white ones that might be mistaken in the trenches as signals of surrender.

Frank was now a member of Kitchener's Mob, or the PBI (Poor Bloody Infantry). Equipped for mobility and concealment, his standard khaki service dress consisted of a tunic with large pockets, a shirt and trousers, a pair of stout leather ankle boots and a peaked cap. But the quintessential piece of headgear, synonymous with the British Tommy, was years away. What is variously called the 'Brodie' helmet (after its designer), the 'shrapnel' or the 'Tommy' helmet, and later by US troops the 'doughboy', was not patented until 1915. From the outbreak of war in August 1914 until the late summer of 1915, no British combatant went into battle wearing head protection stronger than cloth. Only some Germans had their traditional leather 'pickelhaube' helmet with its distinctive spike sticking out of the top. Otherwise they too mostly wore simple caps. The French would be the first to introduce steel helmets in the summer of 1915 in the form of skullcaps worn under woollen headgear, but mostly the traditional kepi was worn until the Adrian helmet was developed, which was also adopted by the Belgian and Italian armies. The British decided that it was too elaborate for speedy manufacture and that the protection it offered was minimal. Brodie's design, pressed from a single thick sheet of steel gave the helmet added strength and was also quick to manufacture. Delivery of the first 1,000,000 would begin in September 1915, although soldiers wearing the new protective headgear at

22. No.1751 Rifleman Frank Edwards, A Company
London Irish Rifles.

Loos would be a rare sight. The roll-out would be completed by the first week
of July in 1916, in time for the ill-fated Somme offensives.

Attached to Frank's weatherproof web equipment were two leather multi-
pocket ammunition carriers holding 150 rounds. As well as a haversack
containing rations and cutlery, his kitbag contained a spare tunic, trousers, shirt,
socks, underwear and boots. The pack, which during training had been made
rigid with cardboard boxes, now contained an unwieldy greatcoat, mess tins,
washing and shaving equipment, spare clothing and a ground sheet. Together
with an entrenching tool and a bayonet, the load totalled 61 pounds in weight.
The small roundel of vulcanite inscribed with his name, number, regiment and
religion worn around his neck from a piece of string was a grim reality check
of what might prove to be the last evidence of his identity. The khaki-covered
packets described as 'field dressings' also underlined the fragility of his situation.

★ ★ ★

At 8am on 9 March 1915, Frank Edwards found himself aboard a train out of St Albans bound for Southampton. The 47th London Division, of which he was now part, would be the second New Territorial Army Division to be delivered complete to France, following immediately behind the North Midland Division, the 46th. After three hours' travelling, the train reached the docks at Southampton. Having disembarked, the men were then lined up in a large empty shed to receive their first supply of active service rations, comprising tea and sugar, half a pound of bread, biscuits half an inch thick and hard as iron, a one pound tin of jam (to be shared among four men for the day) and small tins of bully beef – an unappetising blend of corned beef and salt. With the threat of German submarine attacks preventing daylight crossings, Kitchener's New Army had to wait until around 9pm that evening before boarding the SS *Queen Alexandra*, the SS *Viper* and the SS *Trelford Hall* for Le Havre. Most of the men were quartered on the bare boards of an exposed deck, although some found softer retreats in coils of rope, while the more enterprising took advantage of the ventilator shafts exhausting warm air from below decks. Others escaped the bitter cold wind under canvas in the ship's lifeboats. As the vessels passed out of Spithead and into the open Channel, so the misty white coastline of England drifted out of view. Thereafter only the searchlight beams of the escorting destroyers broke the inky darkness.

'Every moment brought us nearer to the great adventure' recalled the American writer, James Hall. 'We were "off to the wars" to take our places in the far-flung battle line.' At the outbreak of hostilities, Hall joined the British Army as the 'lone American Expeditionary Force' serving in the 9th Battalion Royal Fusiliers. He would take part in the Battle of Loos and a year later re-enlist as a member of the Lafayette Flying Corps, later incorporated into the United States Air Service. It was during these years that he met Charles Nordhoff, a pilot serving in the same corps, with whom he would go on to co-write *Mutiny on the Bounty*. In 1918 James Hall would be shot down behind the German lines and spend the last six months of the war in a prison camp. His war memoirs published in 1916 under the title *Kitchener's Mob and High Adventure* paints a highly evocative picture of life in the trenches as it was lived, told in the often comic, but highly respectful, vernacular of the Londoners around him:

> Here was Romance, lavishly offering gifts dearest to the hearts of Youth, offering them to clerks, barbers, tradesmen, drapers' assistants, men who had never known an adventure more thrilling than a holiday excursion to the Isle of Man or a week of cycling in Kent. Tommy shoulders his rifle and departs for the four corners of the world on a 'bloomin' fine little 'oliday!' A railway journey and a sea voyage in one! 'Blimey! Not 'arf bad, wot?' Perhaps he is stirred at the thought of fighting

23. James Hall.

for 'England, Home, and Beauty.' Perhaps he does thrill inwardly, remembering a sweetheart left behind. But he keeps it jolly well to himself. He has read me many of his letters home, some of them written during an engagement, which will figure prominently in the history of the great World War.

As one of very few Americans starting out on this perilous journey, James Hall was struck by a moment that he could describe only as being 'thoroughly English' in the form of two destroyers laid on to guide the transport across the Channel. He felt that this was so characteristic of the history of these islands and its turbulent relationship with Europe.

Novelist-in-waiting, Geoffrey Belton Cobb, was riding the same waves towards France as Hall. Cobb was then a sales director for Longman's publishers and a regular contributor to *Punch* and other magazines. From 1936 to 1971 he would go on write over fifty detective novels and become a member of the celebrated Detection Club, which included Agatha Christie, Dorothy L. Sayers and G. K. Chesterton. Members of this club would agree to adhere to a code of ethics in their writing so as to give the reader a fair chance at guessing the guilty party. Cobb's first published book, however, was to be the semi-autobiographical *Stand to Arms*, an account of his time as a rifleman with the London Irish Rifles from training through to returning home wounded after the Battle of Loos. Adhering to the strict censorship laws in place, Cobb invented the 'King's Own Eatonshire Regiment (T.F.), entering into the fictional military register his alter ego of No.29876, Private Allan Webb:

> A year ago, Allan was at school, reciting the paradigms of Histini and Tithemi in the Upper Fifth Class Room, bowling googlies for the Second Eleven, and turning out on Thursday afternoons to be drilled by the Sergeant-Major of the Cadet Corps.

Unlike other disguised accounts published during the war, Cobb's coyness did not extend to the complete exclusion of his real regiment. In the flyleaf he has himself down as 'formerly of the London Irish Rifles'.

Yet another prolific writer of detective novels sailing for France at that time was Cecil John Charles Street of the Royal Garrison Special Reserve, whom the celebrated crime writer and student of detective fiction, Julian Symons, described as a prominent member of the 'humdrum' school, a sizeable group of British crime writers with little talent over and above the construction of riddles or crossword puzzles. Also writing under the name of John Street and producing an enduring series as John Rhode, featuring forensic scientist Dr Priestley, one of the first investigators after Sherlock Holmes to embrace the scientific detection of crime, Street wrote four novels under the *non de plume* of Cecil Waye.

As Miles Burton, Street created another long-running series featuring investigator Desmond Merrion, an amateur detective assisting Scotland Yard and his works of non-fiction would go on to include *The Administration of Ireland, Hungary and Democracy*, the translations of Daniel Halvey's *Vauban, Builder of Fortresses* and Maurice Thiery's *The Life and Voyages of Captain Cook*. Writing under the pseudonym, 'F.O.O.' (Forward Observation Officer), C. J. C. Street would provide a vivid blow-by-blow account of the four-day preliminary bombardment of Loos, followed by the day of the assault and the aftermath. His book *With The Guns* was published in 1916, but it would not be until 2005 and its reprinting that his identity was revealed. Later that same year, as part of a talk to the Henry Williamson Society entitled 'The Literary Alchemy of the Battle of Loos', Ian Walker made the further connection with Henry Williamson as the anonymous friend of the writer, who used much of Street's material to follow the fortunes of his fictional hero Phillip Maddison at Loos in *A Fox Under My Cloak*.

★ ★ ★

24. C. J. C. Street.

The 'Channel voyage' as James Hall described the crossing into France, was mercifully uneventful. The three vessels kept fifty yards abreast of each other during the entire journey with the two destroyers keeping guard either side. The U–Boat menace was another dreaded feature punctuating this modern war, but thus far thousands of troops and tons supplies had been transported safely across the Channel without incident. Nevertheless the lifeboats were made ready for immediate launch and all men were provided with life jackets. Another vital piece of kit was *Tommy Atkins's French Manual*, designed to offer a basic understanding of the French 'and their strange language', which would succeed only in the creation of a mangled combination of the two languages that became known as 'Fronglaise'. Also on the required reading list was a copy of Lord Kitchener's first and only personal communiqué with his troops, in which he pronounced:

You are ordered abroad as a soldier of the King to help our French comrades against the invasion of a common enemy. You have to perform a task, which will need your courage, your energy, and your patience. Remember that the honour of the British Army depends upon your individual conduct. It will be your duty not only to set an example of discipline and perfect steadiness under fire, but also to maintain the most friendly relations with those whom you are helping in this struggle. The operations in which you are engaged will, for the most part, take place in a friendly country, and you can do your own country no better service than in showing yourself, in France and Belgium, in the true character of a British soldier. Be invariably courteous, considerate, and kind. Never do anything likely to injure or destroy property, and always look upon looting as a disgraceful act. You are sure to meet with a welcome and to be trusted; and your conduct must justify that welcome and that trust. Your duty cannot be done unless your health is sound. So keep constantly on your guard against any excesses. In this new experience you may find temptations both in wine and women. You must entirely resist both temptations, and while treating all women with perfect courtesy, you should avoid any intimacy. Do your duty bravely. Fear God. Honor the King. KITCHENER, Field-Marshal.

Chapter Four

France

At 4am on 10 March 1915, Frank Edwards arrived at Le Havre, stepping foot on foreign soil for the first time in his life. The trip from Southampton had taken seven hours. Today's ferry services operate to and from Portsmouth. A night crossing takes about the same time as it did 93 years ago. Bar a couple of weeks, Frank's ship docked exactly 500 years after Henry V asked the Great Council to sanction war with France, which they did on 19 April 1415. Historically it's a matter of debate whether Le Havre is a completely new town, or not. The port city was originally built on the orders of François I in 1517 to replace the ancient ports of Harfleur and Honfleur, then silting up, and its name changed to Le Havre (The Harbour), a port town that would become no stranger to war. Harfleur is the setting for Henry V's rousing cry: 'Once more unto the breach, dear friends, once more; or close the wall up with our English dead'. Then, the English had arrived to expel the French and the town was made an English colony until it was reclaimed in 1435.

The area of St Francois was laid out from 1541 in a grid-pattern, which along with Notre-Dame to the west, formed the heart of the new town. Twenty-one years later and Louis I, Prince of Condé, the commander of the Huguenot Army, delivered the town to the custody of Elizabeth I of England, only for the English to be expelled again by Charles IX and Catherine de Medici in 1563. Le Havre became the principal trading post of France's northern coast, prospering especially during the American War of Independence, importing cotton, sugar and tobacco. Under Napoleon III (1852–1870) the town's fortifications were torn down when it started to absorb neighbouring communes.

When British troops embarked half a century later, it was then the European home of the great luxury liners, which continued until the Second World War when the city suffered heavier damage than any other port in Europe. What few churches and other relics of the old city have survived those turbulent times

25. On French soil.

are integrated into the endless panorama of residential blocks, thrown up as economically and swiftly as possible in the spirit of architect Auguste Perret's dictum that 'concrete is beautiful'. Only now, as these words are written, is the largest port in France after Marseilles benefiting from a multi-million pound regeneration project aimed at turning its docklands quarter into a cultural and commercial hub, with the smart bars and apartments replacing factories and warehouses, a familiar scenario to any Londoner stepping off the ferry today.

Alan H. Maude, the Editor of the 47th (London) Division history, records that the men were thoroughly glad to get to France after months of winter training in the soggy fields about London, continually cursed at by their training officers. But now these same men were soldiers, 'proud of themselves, proud of their unit, and proud of their division'. After breakfast on board ship and with the stores and transport disembarked by 8am, the 1st Battalion London Irish Rifles marched into the town, along streets flanked by tall, fronted buildings and filled with women in shawls and bonnets busy buying food from the market stalls.

A few old men and boys sat around smoking and French soldiers could still be seen in their long blue coats and brilliant scarlet trousers from a different age. As Frank and his more sombre khaki-clad contemporaries marched a mile along the seafront – on the right hand side of the road instead of the left – there were no cheers of welcome for the conquering heroes as was expected. The decorations had long gone from the buildings together with any sense of excitement in the air. The euphoria of the first few months of the war had by now faded with British troopships landing with the regularity of the tides. It would only be later and closer to the front that the French civilians would show any enthusiasm for the English soldiers who had come to rid their land of the Germans.

A mile or so inland from the sea, rows of canvas tents and wooden huts comprised the Rest, or Base Camp where meticulous inspections of kit and equipment took place until late at night before the men were allowed to turn in, fourteen to a tent. Following inspection the next morning and as part of General Nugent's brigade, the 1st Battalion marched to the station for the noon train to Cassel, the high ground where General Haig had his headquarters during the key battles of Flanders and from where the German advance was halted. The Ypres Salient would be where some of the most infamous battles of the First World War would be fought and Neuve Chapelle the first large scale organised attack thus far undertaken by the British Army.

In many respects a precursor to Loos, the French commander-in-chief, General Joffre, considered it vital that the Allied forces should take every advantage of their growing numbers and strength on the Western Front, both to relieve German pressure on Russia and if possible to break through in France. The British commander, Sir John French, agreed, believing that it was time to take the offensive after moths of attrition. Joffre looked to overturn the earlier German advance by attacking at the extreme points in Artois and the Champagne district. In particular, if the railways in the Plain of Douai could be recaptured, the Germans would be forced to evacuate large swathes of occupied ground. It was this thinking that shaped most of the actions in the British sector throughout 1915, including the run up to Loos. The attack at Neuve Chapelle was undertaken without the French who were waiting on extra British divisions to relieve them at Ypres. The British losses in the four attacking Divisions were 544 officers and 11,108 other ranks killed, wounded and missing, with roughly comparable German losses.

The journey to Cassel was by way of windowless cattle trucks, each capable of holding forty men or eight horses, complete with provisions and bundles of straw to be spread about the floor. Each man slotted into what meagre space was available before the train set off at a steady eight miles an hour. The only highlights of the painfully slow and uncomfortable journey were meal times, which consisted of beef, jam and biscuits, and water. Travelling north, the men had no real idea of where they were or where they were bound. When it grew dark the doors were closed, which made the cramped interior pitch black and stuffy. If the doors were left open then the cold night air chilled everyone to the bone. There was one stop late in the evening for hot coffee and what is today more delicately termed as a 'comfort break'. Otherwise the train limped along for hour after hour until eventually arriving at Abbeville, another medieval town badly bombed during the Second World War, but with many architectural treasures surviving. Not that there would have been much time for sightseeing in 1915.

Something of a topographical rarity, this tiny hilltop town of Cassel had been much fought over since Roman times, and it was to the top of this hill that the Grand Old Duke of York marched his 10,000 men, a touch of irony that went perhaps unnoticed by the men of the London Irish whose barracks in Chelsea bore his name. Despite its strategic importance, much of the town remains as Frank and his companions would have seen it. The Flemish Grand Place, lined with magnificent mansions from which narrow cobbled streets fan out to the ramparts, and the unrivalled view over Flanders, with Belgium just ten kilometres away. The train pulled in at 9.30am and the men were then marched the seven-and-a-half kilometres to Winnezeele, another tiny village 43 kilometres north-west of Lille and about 25 kilometres south-south-east of Dunkirk. Its churchyard today accommodates a Commonwealth Grave plot where a small number of mostly unidentified casualties from both world wars are commemorated.

Marching from the railway station, Belton Cobb has his man, Allan Webb, forever encountering 'laughing-eyed Irishmen' breaking off to sing 'By Killarney's Lakes and Fells' and later 'for appearances sake' attempting 'Emerald Isle and Winding Bays' only to 'choke over the words bringing tears to their eyes'. For most, however, it may have been the cramp and the fatigue of the long and tedious train journey that provoked such dramatic displays of melancholy, that and the climb up the long steep hill under a blazing hot sun that doubled the weight of a 60-pound pack, rifle and ammunition. To the battle-hardened veterans encountered en route the solution was simple; to dump most of it. A knife could be stuck in the top of one puttee and a spoon in the other. One bar of soap, a towel, a pencil, writing paper and a fork could all be shared with each man taking an individual item. Essential requirements included an overcoat, waterproof sheet, a spare pair of socks and a razor. Everything else could go into the ditch.

Eventually billeted in a barn, Frank Edwards tucked into his ration of beef, bread and jam, supplemented with some butter, cheese and Oxo. In the distance he would have spotted on the far horizon little roundels of cloud in the sky that were constantly appearing and then fading away. This, the new men were informed, was where the trenches lay and the little roundels of cloud were bursts of smoke from German shells.

The next day the Brigade was taken by motor bus to Hazebrouck, which was just another small Flanders market town before it became an important railway junction in the 1860s. Of strategic military importance in the two world wars, many British soldiers are buried in the cemeteries around the town. A private chapel, now part of the College Saint-Jacques, was used as the English hospital during the First World War when parked outside were flotillas of B-Type London omnibuses. Each battalion occupied 42 of these famous transports affectionately known as 'Old Bill'. Skilfully manoeuvred by Cockney drivers unused to the open countryside, but well versed in negotiating tricky roads by naphtha lamps in the pouring rain, they delivered and collected their loads 'with unfailing regularity and punctuality.' Within two days of the outbreak of war, 300 of these vehicles complete with 330 drivers and crew were sent to France and Belgium.

Geoffrey Belton Cobb recalls marching to the nearest main road where thirty of these iconic people carriers were drawn up, painted grey and looking badly knocked about. In single-file, 32 men clambered into each bus with no one allowed on top until the inside was full. The prime position was up top, as packs could be taken off and put under the seat instead of being worn or held on the knees as inside. The downside was the low lying army telephone wires that were strewn across the roads, capable of decapitating the unwary. This odd procession would have presented as strange a sight to any Londoner as were the men loaded onto them, clad as they were in newly issued shaggy grey goatskin coats like a bunch of renegades from the Wild West. Despite their khaki uniforms, the conductors, who were retained as part of the crew, behaved exactly as they did 'when collecting fares between London Bridge and Bethnal Green', except they were now on foreign soil and bound for the front line.

From Hazebrouck the Battalion marched to Burbure where it was inspected by General French and a church service was held by the Bishop of London. Here Frank spent his first week in the large cellar of a railway station, parading twice a day for rifle inspections on the platform and eating meals in the ticket office. Although rough, it was a considerable improvement on the previous 48 hours. A small patch of floor was claimed to spread out a waterproof sheet and a nail was driven into the wall overhead upon which to hang equipment. The pack was carefully folded with all the hard items floor-side to make for a serviceable pillow. Blankets would be provided in the winter, otherwise an overcoat and empty sandbags took some of the chill out of the early spring nights. Washing would always prove difficult. Where there was a well, sometimes the owner would padlock it against use by the soldiers, claiming that they tended to drop bits of soap into the water and foul it, or that dirty water was emptied too close to the fresh supply. In coal districts the mines often boasted showers, whereas in agricultural districts, breweries were called upon to supply large tubs and hot water. Although each division had its own laundry situated behind the lines, underclothing was collected, washed and re-issued only every three or four weeks.

So it was in such conditions that the lads from London got used to their new situation in life, set against a backdrop rumble of artillery fire. In the mornings there would be drill and in the evenings free time to explore the town, frequent the little cafes to eat egg and chips and fresh cream cakes, or to drink wine probably for the first time. So near to the front line, it was hard to accept such a close proximity to the harsher realities thus far only read about in newspaper reports or accounts from veterans.

Lectures were given to help the new influx appreciate how trenches came about and their purpose, how centuries before with their limited range cannon needed to be brought up close to a town or castle walls under siege in order to be effective. This made the gunners highly vulnerable to attack from muskets or crossbows, so a deep trench was dug for the guns to be hauled forward in comparative safety. This in turn made the guns vulnerable to a surprise assault by the enemy out to capture them, which then led to the digging of other trenches parallel to the walls to act as cover for a force of infantry ready and waiting to counter any such attack. In 1914 when the enemy massively outnumbered the

26. 'Old Bill' on the roads of France.

British Army, trenches were dug wherever a stand was to be made. Want of tools and the limited time available meant at first that these defences were never more than shallow ditches below a parapet of loose earth. But the tenuous protection they afforded was sufficient in the brief rearguard actions of the retreat from Mons. When this situation was reversed to an advance after the Battle of the Marne, the Germans repaired to a system of pre-prepared, highly sophisticated deep trenches. Such was the protection they afforded, and in order to maintain what ground they had won, the Allies started doing likewise, digging a line of deep trenches opposite those of the Germans. Instead, therefore, of having two great armies opposing each other in the open, they were now concentrated in lines of excavated enclosures running from the North Sea to Switzerland.

Closest to the enemy was the Fire, or firing trench. Fifty yards behind that was a support trench and then as much as three quarters of a mile from the front a reserve trench. All were linked with communication trenches. Should the enemy succeed in breaking through the first line, there awaiting the interlopers were strong posts at intervals along the line in the form of a square or circular trench fortification with elaborate entanglements and machine-guns. These strongholds were called redoubts or 'keeps', harping back to the days of castles and serving the same purpose in defending at all costs. Posted on the walls of villages close to the firing line were instructions to civilians about how to survive within the shelling zone. This was an area divided into four sections. No Man's Land was what it said on the tin. There was ground open only to those who worked the land or had official business there, another zone open to all who cared to run the risk of the shells and a section that contained the battered villages used for Brigade Reserve.

New arrivals underwent a 24-hour induction, during which time they would learn the routine from experienced men who would share their hard-won knowledge of exactly what to do and how to do it in order to survive not only the enemy but the rigours of trench life. Geoffrey Belton Cobb used his fictional alter-ego, Rifleman Allan Webb, to evoke the sickness, dread and fear on making the first journey into this mythical, menacing place. As a rule the men were marched out after dark. On reaching a village on the Trench Road they were divided into small parties. According to the number of empty houses available they were billeted in the cellars, the ground floor, first floor and the attic. Where the shelling was frequent only the cellar was utilised. Villages closer to the firing line were little more than piles of bricks and shattered furniture strewn about a sea of craters. Yet, remarkably, many of these buildings were still inhabited by old men, women and children battle-hardened to the sound of enemy shells making their way towards them. Patrick MacGill, the self-proclaimed Navvy poet and stretcher-bearer with the London Irish, described the sound of shelling as 'like that of a cartload of rubble being shot down a staircase'.

A mile beyond the town the new arrivals halted at a crossroads. The first 25 men, or half platoon, went on ahead. When they had gone 200 yards the second half followed and so it continued for the 1,000 or so men stretched out in a long procession of small groups 200 yards apart. The reason for this was that they were now well within the range of ordinary enemy artillery fire and less vulnerable as a single column to the occasional shell landing amongst them. Talking and smoking were strictly forbidden as these columns made their way along the roads. In shallow pits, batteries of Allied artillery lay hidden under the boughs of trees and brushwood, wrapped in sheeting to protect them from the weather. Guides were on hand to lead the newcomers off the road and down narrow lanes, through the remains of houses and along any circuitous route able to foil German snipers. Hand painted signposts offered directions 'TO THE WAR', 'TO LONDON' and 'TO BERLIN'. Although many a trench had been dug during training, the 'real thing' was somewhat different. Entered by a flight of steps cut from the hard chalk soil, the excavation was often no more than three feet wide at the top, to around two-and-a-half feet at the base and about six feet below the level of the ground. As if in a maze following a zigzagging course, nothing could be seen but the rough-hewn walls either side with a gap of sky above. Loosely fastened to the walls or in the slushy floor underfoot, a mass of telephone wires threatened to trip up the unwary. This was the communication trench, which eventually gave way to the reserve trench and then possibly a clearing where other trenches met in different directions wryly signposting Piccadilly Circus, Regent Street or Oxford Circus.

Unlike the other trenches, the fire trench was much broader. To all intents and purposes it also ran straight and therefore vulnerable to bursting shrapnel shells or end to end (enfiladed) fire if overrun. To counter this, bastions of earth (or traverses) were left every four or five yards, dividing the trench into a number of shorter trenches, or bays, themselves connected by the narrower communication trenches. Because of their depth, what were known as firesteps, measuring about two feet high and eighteen inches wide, were cut into the side of the trench facing the enemy. All the earth dug to create this forward warren was put into fabric bags to create a bullet-proof parapet thirty inches thick and up to twenty inches high.

Perhaps the most unnerving feature was the close proximity of the enemy, sometimes only 250 yards away. At night a flare thrown up would show the new men the lay of the land beyond the sandbags. First a blinding explosion from an oversized brass pistol sent a ball of light high up into the night sky like a rocket. When it touched the ground it flared up in the grass, illuminating everything around it for thirty yards. Clearly silhouetted in the foreground was the British wire entanglement and in the distance that of the German defences, each designed to protect against night raiding parties.

27. A ball of light sailing into the
air like a rocket. (Ruth Cobb)

During the daylight hours, Frank Edwards and his fellow inductees were advised of the single most important rule, to keep the head down. Failure to do so meant an easy kill for a sniper. In addition to this, new arrivals were instructed to always wear woollen helmets or 'stocking caps' to baffle the outline of a stiff cap. On watch duty, the 'hour down', as distinguished from the 'hour up', would be spent sitting or lying on the fire-step. Although officers were on more intimate terms with the men on the firing line, discipline was relaxed only in so far as the men were not required to salute. Sentries were given a periscope made from a thin metal tube about eighteen inches long with a sloped piece of mirror fixed at either end with slots as windows. The tube was wrapped in sacking to camouflage it from the sandbags where the upper mirror was held a few inches above the parapet. Reflected in the lower mirror was a panorama of all that separated the two armies. The static display of British entanglements gave way to a long stretch of grass ending at the enemy's wire barricade and their parapets beyond.

Throughout the hour on duty only a confirmed sighting of the enemy was to be met with immediate fire. Otherwise the position was not to be exposed. Any sleep would be taken on the fire-step, although in reality the constant noise of pot shots loosed off by sentries on either side made that rarely possible. There was no leaving the bay or going into a dugout. All equipment was kept on and

28. Through the periscope, a view over No Man's Land. (Ruth Cobb)

buckled. The bandolier slung across the chest containing fifty extra rounds of ammunition was to be used first. The rounds in the equipment pouches were there for emergencies. Frank's outmoded rifle was to be kept loaded with a round in the breech, ready to be fired. Backpacks and water bottles could be taken off and piled into a small hollow in the trench wall.

Required to stand by for immediate support, the night was spent fully clothed, including boots and puttees. This was one of the strictest of trench rules and the one that caused most discomfort. The removal of any clothes was forbidden, except for the tunic, which might be taken off in hot weather, provided the equipment was immediately put on again next to the shirt. The reasoning being that it would not do for a man to be caught with his pants down when the Germans made a surprise attack. Puttees were strips of brown cloth wound round the ankles to provide support and waterproofing, but these failed miserably in respect of the latter. After a night of rain when the floor of the trench became flooded, the puttees soaked into the socks, which dried uncomfortably slowly. Over ten to fourteen days the results would provide a great deal of work for the medical officer. After several months in France, men that had arrived fit and well found themselves in hospital for one reason or another, more often suffering from the appalling effects of trench foot, a terrible infection caused by cold, wet and unsanitary conditions. In an interview after the war, sergeant Harry Roberts of the Lancashire Fusiliers described the condition thus:

Your feet swell to two or three times their normal size and go completely dead. You could stick a bayonet into them and not feel a thing. If you are fortunate enough not to lose your feet and the swelling begins to go down, it is then that the intolerable, indescribable agony begins. I have heard men cry and even scream with the pain and many had to have their feet and legs amputated.

Particularly problematical in the winter of 1914–15 when over 20,000 men were treated for this miserable condition, the only remedy was to dry the feet and change socks several times a day. It would not be until the end of 1915 that British soldiers were issued with three pairs of socks and strict orders to change them at least twice a day. They were also ordered to cover their feet with grease made from whale oil, estimated at ten gallons per day per battalion.

At dawn and sunset, the hours when attacks were most likely, sentries would 'Stand To [Arms]'. The order to 'Stand Down' was issued when it was clear there would be no enemy assault. The day sentries posted was followed by morning inspection by the corporal. Despite a profound lack of sleep the trench would be scraped as clean as a barrack room, spent cartridges collected and put into a special bag kept for the purpose and the Fire Step and floor swept using a broom made out of a stick and an empty sandbag. Breakfast at 06.00 hours consisted of hot bacon and tea brought from the cookhouse which was maintained in the last village behind the lines. Its delivery was usually accompanied by a bout of shellfire that lasted until about 08.00 hours. After breakfast and with everything spick and span, the night sentry could creep into a dugout to sleep.

Dugouts were often little more than a hollow cut into the trench wall with a timber-shored roof. Measuring five-and-a-half feet long by four-and-a-half feet high, each chamber was meant to contain four men at one time, making sleep for anyone above average height especially difficult, and in full equipment including the 60-round band of ammunition digging into the ribs, near impossible. The comfort of trenches depended entirely on the number and conditions of dugouts it had. Some dugouts were shallow caves where one man might curl up uncomfortably. Others were fairly roomy with substantial walls. Some had no roofs except for a waterproof sheet. The best trenches were invariably those dug by the French, some of which were near palatial, as much as six feet wide and high and eighteen feet long, big enough to accommodate an entire section. The roofs were supported by stout wooden uprights and cross beams covered with sandbags and earth. Sometimes these dugouts were furnished with tables and chairs and mattresses relieved from deserted houses.

Only hard experience would allow Frank to know when he was the target of an incoming shell or one intended for a target miles away. Shells were divided into four main classes: high explosive, shrapnel, high explosive shrapnel and 'whizz-bangs'. The latter were fired from a small gun placed in the German

29. Dinner in the trenches.

front trench. It travelled so fast that the sound of its approach became lost in the louder noise of the explosion, giving no warning of its arrival, except for a 'whizz' and then a 'bang'. High explosives were capable of destroying masonry or buildings. The small metal fragments from high explosive shrapnel, generally triggered by a time fuse fifty feet above the ground, scattered over an area of 12,000 square yards. Often it burst on impact. 'Minnies' were trench mortars filled with an explosive powerful enough to destroy dugouts and sections of trench. As the name suggests, rifle grenades were small bombs attached to steel rods that were fired out of rifles. Like hand grenades they were exploded by a time fuse and were intended to injure personnel rather than destroy infrastructure. The advantage of bombs over shells – according to the recipients – was that they were slower and could be seen coming in. By night they left a trail of sparks. Frank Edwards would soon become adept at crying out 'Bomb right!' or 'Bomb left!'

Although both sides employed these weapons, the German '*minenwerfer*' trench mortar bomb was answered with the British aerial torpedo, a large bomb fired out of a trench mortar and fitted with 'wings' like an arrow to ensure it landed on its explosive tip. Then there was mining, where a shaft might be sunk for thirty feet or so and a tunnel cut towards the enemy lines with a second tunnel parallel, but about forty feet directly below it. The heavy charges placed at intervals along this second tunnel were fired by a fuse, often preceding an infantry attack. If the enemy discovered a shaft coming their way then a small charge could be placed to destroy the works but not disturb the trenches above.

★ ★ ★

At the end of their 24-hour seasoning, Frank and his comrades were marched out and back along the Trench Road under the cover of darkness. After midnight when they reached their billet in a ruinous village there would be a welcome mug of tea before the bugles sounded Lights Out. Having earned a good sleep, breakfast was not until about 11.00 hours and then after a brief kit and equipment inspection, leave was granted to go into town. Pay was issued as nearly as possible every fortnight, the usual amount being in the region of five francs (just over 20p) with the rest of the seven shilling pay (35p) each week obtainable on return to England. Although not a fortune by any stretch of the imagination, with a tour of duty in the trenches allowing for a certain amount to be accumulated, there was usually enough to have a reasonable celebration when returning to the billets.

Despite all the obvious difficulties, local women continued for the most part to do a roaring trade selling coffee, eggs, fried potatoes and bread and butter, far preferable to the slop provided by the company field-kitchen. These two-wheeled carts contained a fire and five large metal pots, known as 'Dixie's', each holding enough tea or stew for fifty men. The fire was spread along the floor of the kitchen so that everything could be cooked together when a company went into the trenches. If a communication trench was fairly short, hot meals were cooked and carried to the troops by fatigue parties. Dry stores, such as bread, biscuits, jam and cheese, were distributed separately. For breakfast, each man received tea, bread or biscuits, jam and a rasher of bacon. Dinner was always a stew made of bully beef mixed with some fresh meat, potatoes and possibly carrot or onion thrown in. A particularly unappetising dish at the best of times, it was made all the worse after a slow journey of nearly two miles by which time it had become a congealed and greasy mess.

Where there was no village close to the line and the communication trenches were extra long, then meat was sent down raw for cooking on site. Although tedious and dangerous, as the even the slightest whiff of smoke might be greeted with a hail of shellfire, this was a welcome opportunity to cook something more appetising. Charcoal might be used to cut down on the smoke, but wood, wherever it was found, was chopped down into small pieces with an entrenching tool and carried under the flaps of packs ready to take to the trenches.

A certain amount of filtered water was carried up every night by reserve troops, but when this was exhausted supplies had to be found elsewhere, from a well or garden pump nearby, which would inevitably become the target of enemy sniper and shellfire. Rainwater was also harnessed for drinking but not washing, so men stayed filthy for days, which was preferable to going thirsty. Tea left over from breakfast was used for shaving water.

The major blot on the landscape when returning from the front, however, was drill. Parade was called for at 06.30 hours each morning for half an hour's smart marching and running. At 08.30 hours the battalion paraded again, this time four hours drill in marching order wearing full packs. In the afternoon there was either more drill or a route march. Occasionally a half day respite was granted where the men were allowed to roam around the town or to play cricket or football. The only limitations imposed was that no one could go further than three-quarters of a mile from his headquarters and everyone was to be ready to march to the firing line at one hour's notice by day or thirty minutes at night.

The 47th Division was now ready to take charge of a section of firing line. Every fourth day two of its brigades would be sent forward to relieve weary comrades in the firing trench who would march back in town five hours later. The remainder, including the 1st Battalion London Irish Rifles, were mostly kept at Brigade Reserve where a whole host of fatigue duties were on offer to keep the large numbers of men fit, sharp and alert.

A never ending procession of Army Service Corps' wagons ferried stores to and from the nearest village to the trenches. The boxes of rifle ammunition and bombs were exceedingly heavy. Although manageable slung between two men on the open road, in the confines of a narrow trench it was a backbreaking task. Precious supplies of filtered water were contained in large earthenware jars, carried two to a man along the trenches by means of loops of string tied round the neck, which cut into the hands as the jars dragged along the trench walls. If drawn as part of a digging party, then Frank would parade in the street at dusk armed with a pick, a shovel and his rifle before the company filed down into the trenches to collect rubbish for burial in a large refuse pit out in the open. Provided the work was done swiftly and silently, the danger of being spotted or heard was low. Overhead in the hours of daylight there might be a kite-balloon used for observation, or an enemy aeroplane trying to spot a sea of white faces looking up, presenting an ideal target. Such a threat was alleviated with the order of 'Heads down and faces to the ground!' Then there was the task of improving the trenches and the stock of sandbags.

Following the aftermath of an artillery bombardment, Frank might form part of a working party tasked with going out at night into No Man's Land to fix the smashed entanglements. Unlike work at the rubbish pit, which was at least between the British lines, there was nothing to separate the workmen and the enemy. Standing upright, the engineers in charge barked orders regardless. At training camp in England, Frank had learned how to drive wooden stakes into mud with special muffled hammers, but the tricky task of attaching the lethally sharp barbed wire was made no easier with the thought of a rocket flare revealing his figure silhouetted in the inky darkness. Rifle, machine-gun fire, or even artillery might at any moment replace the sound of constant tapping taking place between both sets of lines.

One of the most risky and uncomfortable of the night operations was that of patrols, looking for Germans hiding in No Man's Land. This involved lying down in the damp grass for hours at a time listening for any sign of enemy activity. Daytime duties might involve taking part in a dummy assault. Here, the short ladders used to climb out of the trenches would be conspicuously propped up to show their upper rungs above the parapet, which immediately attracted a shower of German bullets. To add to the deception, mock assault troops would march along the fire trench with their gleaming bayonets raised sufficiently high, then dash back unseen via the support trench to recreate the scene as though they were a fresh platoon. Despite this lack of subtlety, such a ploy would often attract a full-blown bombardment of artillery and machine-gun fire while the real assault went ahead elsewhere with relatively little opposition.

According to the war diaries of Sgt H. J. Warren MM, 1st Battalion London Irish Rifles, the first time the regiment came under fire was at Cambrin, a small farming and light industrial village about 24 kilometres north of Arras and eight kilometres east of Bethune on the road to La Bassée. At one time, Cambrin housed brigade headquarters and until the end of the war was only ever about 800 metres from the front line trenches. Its military cemetery, often called Cambrin Chateau Cemetery, was begun in February 1915 and contains many graves of those fallen in the Battle of Loos. It was used as a front line cemetery until December 1918. The London Irish Rifles marched off to the firing line in the Cambrin brickfields on 8 April 1915 and appear to have encountered little in the way of action. Sydney (later Sir Sydney) Sadler, another sergeant in the London Irish, recalls this was more of a move designed to mix with more seasoned troops where the regiment spent 48 hours in the enemy-held brickfields. Here the Germans used stacks of bricks for machine-gun emplacements, 'quite formidable shelters – we were unable to dislodge them, as intense bombardment was necessary, and unfortunately we were very short of shells and armament.'

With time spent both for division or brigade alternately in reserve and in the front line, days were spent mostly making improvements to the trench. The evenings were devoted to writing letters or reading newspapers and magazines. Books required more concentration and so were deemed less suitable. Games were also forbidden for the same reason. Cigarettes were smoked at all times of the day and night, except on sentry duty. The chief excitement of the day was the arrival of the post brought by carts to the last village, which was sorted by a postman supplied to each company.

After about a fortnight of this Frank's battalion moved off again. The chief effect of these movements was for the men to be made aware of differing local conditions where sometimes it was a matter of constantly dodging shells and elsewhere, such as at Cambrin, it might be quiet for weeks at a time. The Battalion then found itself in reserve at Richbourg, returning to Béthune on 12 May, three days before the British assault. An attractive and bustling town, Béthune is situated between Arras and St Omer just off the A26 motorway. The main square features a mixture of neo-regional, art deco and, central to the scheme of things in northern France, the omnipresent belfry. Almost of all the square was rebuilt after 1918 when the town's citizens were awarded the Croix de Guerre and Légion d'Honneur for their part in the First World War. On 16 May 1915, the Germans blew up a mine in front of the London Irish, but no follow up attack was made. Just as he had learned from his trench induction, so Frank Edwards was able to hear German sappers burrowing beneath his feet.

Four days later, the 1/18th London was relieved by 20th Battalion and returned to billets. Sometime before 27 May, with Lieutenant Colonel E. G. Concanon DSO, in command, the regiment was 'blooded' at Festubert, a tiny farming village in the Ypres Salient, one of several unsuccessful attempts to take the formidable Aubers Ridge. Sergeant Sadler recalled a difficult terrain where it was not possible to dig trenches, only to build sandbag breastworks with no shelter behind, similar to the conditions at Neuve Chapelle: 'At dawn stand-to we had our first experience of the ravages of war. Apparently, the Indian Division had attacked at this point and there had been terrible slaughter.' Forming part of the French commander-in-chief's Artois spring offensive, this was the second large-scale infantry assault following the earlier attack on Neuve Chapelle. The British were joined by Canadian and Indian troops in a response to pressure applied by 'Papa' Joffre, as the commander-in-chief was known. In what would become a familiar scenario, the attack around the village of Festubert was preceded by a four day artillery bombardment of over 400 guns firing 100,000 shells that failed to destroy the German front line defences. Despite this, initial rapid progress was made by the Indian infantry. A further assault by Canadian troops, however, proved unsuccessful and as Allied troops tried to consolidate the meagre gains made thus far, the Germans managed to reinforce their front line.

Renewed attacks by Allied forces between 20 and 24 May saw the eventual capture of Festubert village itself, but at a cost of some 16,000 casualties for an advance of less than one kilometre. By now, rifleman Frank Edwards and

30. An early trench.

his companions harboured no misconceptions about the war and how it was to be fought. They were seasoned veterans of front line service, even if full combat experience was waiting in the wings. Since their arrival in France back in March, the supply and medical services had worked smoothly and efficiently, with the men of the 47th Division having every reason to consider themselves much better provided for than other units they came across. Throughout the summer until late September, Frank and his comrades took alternate spells in the line with reserve duties and working parties. They were as prepared as any for what would be their finest hour close to another unremarkable French town about to secure its place in history.

Chapter Five

The Big Push

In early June 1915 the French handed over part of their line to the British from La Bassée Canal (or the Canal d'Aire) running west–east southward to Lens, which comprised a sector overlooking the small mining village of Loos. After much confusion with the suburb of Lille, which to this day looms larger on the map of northern France, the region's name (Goghelle) was added in 1937. Variously known as Lothae, Lo, Lohes, Loes, Loez, the name 'Loos' was officially sanctioned in 1791, derived either from the German or Dutch word for wood. With no archaeological evidence of a forest, the alternative derivation of 'Laupo', meaning a marshy meadow, better suits the topography of the place. Dating back at least to the sixth century, by the Middle Ages Loos was a large farming community, becoming prosperous in the mid-nineteenth century with the discovery of coal. The town was completely destroyed during the First World War, with not a single building or tree unaffected by the carnage and little remaining of its past. Nowadays, Loos-en-Gohelle hosts light industry, but also retains its rural heritage in the form of some thirty farms.

In 1915 the setting was a huddle of densely packed mining villages set between giant slagheaps and massive pithead structures. The Loos battlefield lies immediately north of the mining town of Lens, in the heart of this once thriving industrial area of north-east France where the ground is flat, offering a decidedly difficult challenge for any attacking army. The Official History sums up the area as a more unpromising scene for a great offensive battle than can hardly be imagined, the surface a barren prairie of rank grass intersected by trenches whose white chalk parapets defied concealment.

It was around 1870 that the district – previously poor agricultural land – had been opened up to coal mining. There were several principal pitheads within the battle area as well as a large number of auxiliary shafts (or *puits*) each of considerable wartime tactical importance. The pitheads themselves comprised tall rectangular iron latticed towers for the lift shafts, which made for invaluable observation posts across the flat terrain. Also useful from a military perspective were the massive dumps of slag and waste known as *crassier* that still litter the landscape. For a complete and comprehensive description of the lie of the land as it stood within the context of the planned British offensive, readers should seek out Nick Lloyd's book *Loos 1915*. Alternatively, the narrative supplied by Forward Observation Officer Captain C. J. C. Street, in his memoir *With The Guns*, provides a more narrative evocation of the terrain as it presented itself to the New British Army:

> From the La Bassee Canal southward to Souchez is a purely coal-mining district, one of the most important in France, an undulating country devoid of natural features, but abounding in artificial ones, such as chimney-stacks, mine-shafts and dump-heaps. The miners' villages, locally termed 'corons', group themselves about the pit-heads, and form two long lines of almost continuous brick and mortar, separated by a shallow valley, normally under cultivation, but now lying fallow and deserted, varying in width from a few hundred yards to a couple of miles or so. In the centre of this valley lies Loos, a village of some two thousand inhabitants, conspicuous for miles round from the huge double shaft, the famous Pylons that rise nearly three hundred feet above the surface of the plain. Along the course of the valley, ran the two opposing lines with their maze of support, reserve and communication trenches leading up the slopes of the valley to the villages in rear. Well up the western slope of the valley, the village of Loos lay a mile within the lines on the German side. The whole of the southern sector of these parallel works could be plainly seen from the British observation posts in Maroc as great gouges of white chalk excavations cut into the green overgrowth of weeds, behind which rose the twin embankments of deposited slag, or Crassier. The Double Grassier was at the north and the Puits XVI embankment to the south. Both had transformed into highly effective enemy strongholds, creating in their wake the westernmost fortifications of Lens. It was opposite the extremity of the Puits XVI embankment that the Allied armies first met in that great chain that spread with one short gap to the far-away Swiss mountains.

Today, most visitors pass by along the A26 Autoroute from Calais without so much as a hint that the black industrial hills immediately north of Lens shroud the site of the first great land battle fought by the British Army in the First World War. Numbered 11 and 19 by the local mining company, the Double Crassier, so much a feature of the Battle of Loos, have grown from the long, slender heaps held by the Germans into twin mountain-like peaks, visible for miles in all directions. Coal continued to be mined here until 1986, leaving the landscape marked by Europe's largest slagheaps that now represent a valiant marketing opportunity for one of north-west France's dourest zones. A tourist board leaflet optimistically describes the twin 188-metre conical heaps as 'two natural belfries', the 24 million cubic metres of slag hosting guided walking tours, annual drama festivals, paragliding, cycling and orienteering on the bleak slopes. Otherwise this forlorn industrial wasteland, ravaged by two world wars, slashed by motorways and contemporary town planning, offers little incentive to visitors other than those drawn to the battlefields.

East of the town the ground rises almost imperceptibly towards another topographical feature synonymous with the Battle of Loos, Hill 70. The two lines of villages surrounding the mines owned by the Compagnie des Mines de Bethune included Cambrin, Vermelles, Philosophe, Mazin-garbe, Les Brebis, Grenay, Maroc, and Aix Noulette, which in September 1915 were all held by the Allies. The eastern line, consisting of Auchy, Haisnes, Cite St Elie, Hulluch, Benifontaine, Vendin, Cite St Auguste, Lievin and Lens and its suburbs were all under German occupation. Frank Edwards found himself part of the British effort forming the left flank of a massive French offensive north of the town of Arras.

On 4 June 1915, Joseph Joffre, the commander-in-chief, judged this region to be particularly favourable for an all-out attack against the German line. He was tired of German successes. But now, with his army some 200,000 men stronger than it had been in October 1914, the French commander was anxious to mount an assault that would force the enemy to retreat.

The commander of the British Expeditionary Force, Sir John French, was urged to mount an offensive to the north of the French Tenth Army between the towns of Loos and La Bassée. Although he had recently voiced disquiet in the press over the lack of munitions, the British commander now felt the time was right, ordering Sir Douglas Haig, commanding the First Army Corps, to prepare a detailed plan. Haig, however, failed to share the view that the chosen ground was particularly promising for an attack, large or small. With stocks of ammunition still very low, he preferred instead a short attack on an area north of La Bassée canal, towards Violaines and La Bassée with action south of the canal restricted to subsidiary flank attacks. According to Haig:

> The ground, for the most part bare and open, would be so swept by machine-gun and rifle fire both from the German front trenches and from the numerous fortified villages immediately behind them, that a rapid advance would be impossible.

The land was hard chalk, with the long, unprotected upward slopes providing an open arena in which advancing infantry would be effortlessly mown down. When General Sir Henry Rawlinson saw it he announced: 'My front is as flat as the palm of a hand. Hardly any cover anywhere. Attack will cost us dearly, and we shall not get very far.'

British strength on the Western Front was also reduced by the numbers of troops and the amount of equipment and munitions being consumed in the Gallipoli theatre and elsewhere. If such an offensive was to have a reasonable chance of success then it would have to be delivered on a continuous front of no less than 25 miles by a force of at least 36 Divisions supported by 1,500 heavy guns and howitzers. As the British force would not be in this position until the spring of 1916 at the earliest, the prevailing view in the British camp was that that they should maintain a defensive position on the Western Front until that time. However, it was the French who decided who the British attacked, where they attacked and when. The British generals were required only to work out how to do it.

Then there was the tenuous position of the Russians to consider. Lord Kitchener feared how long they could withstand the vigorous German onslaught. He too had favoured a policy of active defence in France until such time as a full complement of British forces had been deployed. But the situation in the east caused him to modify this view, believing that the Allies had to act robustly in order to ease the pressure off Russia. An emphatic victory over the Germans would, he thought, encourage neutral countries to join the

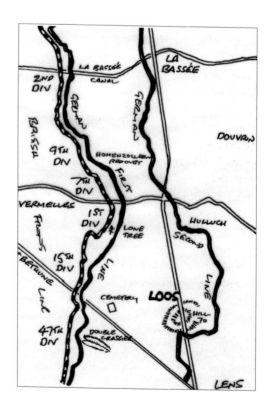

31. Map of the British line, 1915.

Allied cause, which would in turn force the Germans to reduce their operations against the Russians. In this, everything hinged on ensuring that the planned offensive was carried out with a sufficient force adequately resourced.

In Haig's theatre of operations, the Germans had massively strengthened their defences in the area to be attacked. Their three lines had been deepened and were reinforced with extra machine-gun redoubts. Fifteen-yard deep barbed wire was made to a new design that could not be cut by existing British equipment and was beyond the range of the British field artillery. Only when the first line fell could the big guns be advanced, by which time the Germans would have further reinforced the area. The key lesson learned from the spring offensives was the requirement for pre-emptive bombardments of high explosive shells fired by the heaviest artillery to provide gaps for the attacking infantry to break through. By way of a compromise, Joffre agreed to postpone the assault until the end of August 1915, which still left the British forces on the Western Front ill-prepared for a major offensive, with the plan calling for a continuous bombardment by heavy artillery followed by an initial assault of 75,000 British infantry. Such was the dearth of British numbers and heavy artillery to fully support such a breadth of front that the decision was taken for the first time by the Allies to deploy a lethal barrage of chlorine gas.

Dolefully described in the final orders as 'The Accessory', Haig believed that it was the right time for its use. Coupled with the element of surprise for greater effect, its deployment would allow for a large scale attack such as at that planned at Loos. Earlier in 1915, a German prisoner had warned of the first gas attack, which was delayed due to unfavourable wind conditions. In a bulletin dated 30 March, the French Tenth Army noted that the German XV Corps had installed thousands of iron cylinders containing an asphyxiating gas into their front line defences. The German attack when it came comprised the release of 180 tonnes of the poisonous substance in a continuous flow that lasted a full five minutes. The mist that rolled forward on the wind created a breach in the Allied lines over four miles wide, which the Germans were quick to exploit.

Some of the Canadian troops who took the full brunt of the deadly blanket at Givenchy described a peculiar grey, yellow, greenish cloud in colour that was darker nearer the ground and lighter towards the top. The chlorine acted as a powerful irritant on the lungs and mucous membranes, with prolonged exposure proving fatal. To counteract the effect of the gas, German troops were issued with cotton pads dipped in a special solution, but it was only after the second battle of Ypres that the Allies began to put fundamental defences in place. Flannel bags with talc eye-pieces were first issued to machine-gunners, while others had to rely on a piece of gauze or cotton wadding soaked in water for some protection.

Initially, the concept of large concentrations of a poisonous gas was as unfamiliar to the Allies as it was incomprehensible from a practical or moral viewpoint. Experimental research in Britain was carried out with the Kestner-Kellner Alkali Company, the only firm capable of manufacturing chlorine gas in quantity. The final large-scale trials took place near Runcorn in June 1915 where a continuous cloud of compressed gas discharged from cylinders was successfully carried by the wind towards the target positions. Special companies of Royal Engineers were formed, with all men given the rank of 'chemist corporal'. The first two companies, totalling 34 sections of 28 men, were assigned to the First Army for forthcoming operations on 4 September 1915, three weeks before the planned assault at Loos.

★ ★ ★

Having arrived in France in March 1915, it had taken Frank Edwards a full five months by road, train and on foot to arrive in the country's equivalent of England's Black Country. Following this same route was Philip Gibbs, one of the most outstanding British wartime reporters and writers of the day who had spent much of the opening months of the war as a reporter for the *Daily Chronicle*, following armies across northern France in the vain hope of being in the right place to witness events first hand. In his several autobiographies, Gibbs covers extensively his experiences in the First World War.

Realities of War ranks among the first publications responsible for creating the 'Lost Generation' narrative of the 1920s in its condemnation of the futility of war and the incompetence of military leaders. Aside from joining a British volunteer ambulance service on the Ypres front in late 1914, Gibbs had seen very little action. But while other correspondents unashamedly dramatised their reports, he concentrated on the thoughts and fears of the fighting soldiers themselves to vividly describe the battle experience. *The Soul of War* published in 1915 typifies Gibbs's accurate and succinct style, and is clearly sympathetic to the lot of the ordinary Tommy.

In his travels from village to village, Gibbs eventually came across the London Irish, although for reasons of security, he described them as the battalion of the 47th London Division selected to form the first line of attack at Loos. These men, he gleaned, were out

... to win honour for the New Army and old London ... a different crowd from the Scots ... not so hard, not so steel-nerved, with more sensibility to suffering, more imagination, more instinctive revolt against the butchery that was to come.

Moreover, 'they too had been "doped" for morale, their nervous tension had been tightened up by speeches addressed to their spirit and tradition.' The battle to come was to be

> London's day out, a fight for the glory of the old town ... the old town where they had lived in little suburban houses with flower-gardens, where they had gone up by the early morning trains to city offices and government offices and ware-houses and shops, in days before they ever guessed they would go a-soldiering, and crouch in shell-holes under high explosives, and thrust sharp steel into German bowels. But they would do their best. They would go through with it. They would keep their sense of humour and make cockney jokes at death. They would show the stuff of London pride.

Figuratively speaking, Gibbs claimed to know many of these young Londoners, observing them and their daily lives as he had done out and about the capital in the days before the war. One he did know personally, an officer, whom he had watched as a boy playing in Kensington Gardens just a few years before. Now as an observer of war, as he had been a spectator in peacetime, Gibbs wrote movingly of the 47th London Division, going forward to the Battle of Loos, made up of the same men shaped by all the influences, habit, and tradition as he:

> Their cradle had been rocked to the murmurous roar of London traffic. Their first adventures had been on London Commons. The lights along the Embankment, the excitement of the streets, the faces of London crowds, royal pageantry, mar-riages, crownings, burials ... the little dramas of London life, had been woven into the fibre of their thoughts, and it was the spirit of London which went with them wherever they walked in France or Flanders, more sensitive than country men to the things they saw. Some of them had to fight against their nerves on the way to Loos. But their spirit was exalted by a nervous stimulus before that battle, so that they did freakish and fantastic things of courage.

After a fortnight in Corps Reserve, Frank Edwards returned to Maroc (Maroc-Grenay), about fifteen kilometres south east of Béthune. In 1915 it was three miles behind the trenches and where the men were excused parades and drill, as this place was in constant observation by German aeroplanes and if seen, would have been shelled. During the greater part of the war it was a front-line cemetery used by fighting units and field ambulances, protected from German observation by the slight rise in the ground. The Maroc British Cemetery, located in the village of Grenay, was begun by French troops in August 1915 and first used as a Commonwealth cemetery by the 47th (London) Division in

32. Philip Gibbs.

January 1916. It now contains 1,379 Commonwealth burials and commemorations of the First World War, including 87 unidentified officers and men of the London Regiment, killed during the brief capture of Loos.

The first day in reserve was spent in complete idleness with the men wondering what they were doing so near the firing line. They could not be meant for Reserves, as none of their division was in the trenches. Finding himself more rested than usual and in his role as 'a bit of a wag', Frank Edwards led a procession around Maroc where he and his pals had found a stash of frock coats and women's dresses in the wardrobes of deserted homes. It was a temporary respite, however. For just as the farmers fattened their livestock before market, so the men of the first battalion London Irish had been chosen to lead the great charge. In his memoirs, Captain C. J. C. Street recalls throughout August and September the roads behind the Allied front covered by troop and equipment movements and rumour busy with conjecture. He writes of the pessimists maintaining that the British were planning a mere feint with the real advance coming from the French in Champagne. The optimists, he noted, looked at last to the general advance that would see off trench warfare, 'when the Battle of Position shall give way to the Battle of Movement, the beginning of the final struggle that will end only with the death-throes of the enemy on the Rhine!'

Meanwhile the big guns active in the distance would intermittently belch flame and then give out a loud crack before sending a shell screeching through the air to explode on the German trenches.

The London Territorials were kept busy making 'saps' – trenches dug at right angles to the fire trench running in the direction of the enemy, but not as a rule beyond the wire entanglement. Each sap ended in a small round space known as the sap-head, which was furnished with a fire step to be used as an advanced look-out post, or in the event of an attack, to enfilade the advancing enemy. Normally a sap was made cutting through the existing trench wall with a pick, except in this instance it was cut out in the open and dug as a normal trench, regardless of the greater risk of being shelled or sniper shot. The orders were that this task was so essential it had to be completed at all costs. Such an instruction was often issued as a means of ensuring that the work was carried out quickly and efficiently.

On this occasion, however, its urgency was underlined when the whole company was called out at night to dig. From the end of the sap towards the German trenches for 180 yards was a zigzag line of tape previously laid by the engineers, marking where the men were required to dig a communication trench measuring three feet wide and six feet deep. At this point the enemy's trenches were just 900 feet from the British fire trench. Even if the diggers were illuminated by flares or a searchlight and then shelled, the order was to keep on digging. Mercifully, the Germans had no searchlights in that area. They could doubtless hear the men cutting away in the dark but would not have been able to make out where the noise was coming from. Should an enemy patrol come looking for the source then fifty riflemen lay hidden in the grass waiting to intercept.

The soil from the initial cut was placed into sandbags and used to build a top edge to the trench wall, preventing loose earth falling back down. According to Geoffrey Belton Cobb, only one man was killed by a random shot from a sniper. A few shells landed on the trenches behind, but after five hour's work the new trench was half finished and the troops ordered back for an early breakfast and sleep until reveille at eleven. As the hard dried mud was hacked off clothes and equipment, so the men learned that the communication trenches being dug at short intervals along a mile-and-a-half long front were designed to connect to a new fire trench effectively reclaiming a piece of No Man's Land 200 yards closer to the enemy lines. German observers, however, had by now identified the source of the previous night's digging, which saw their guns trained on the location in readiness for the second night. In addition, the soft soil had now given way to hard chalk and no sooner would the first pickaxe clunk into the hard material than the shells would begin to rain down.

The first and only account of the London Irish Rifles at Loos would appear in the popular *Weekly Despatch* newspaper a couple of weeks after the battle.

The correspondent was an unnamed rifleman recovering from his injuries in a hospital bed in London. The days of digging leading up to the great charge he recalled as being accompanied by the angry roar of the enemy's guns raining down bullets and shells as the men worked, with the explosions silhouetting the diggers momentarily every so often. 'How the beggars got the range I can't tell' he sighed. 'They must have got it during the day. But it was deadly accurate, and they picked the men off continually.' Far from hindering progress, however, the onslaught served only to make the men work harder and dig deeper for greater cover:

> All the time – and it is as fine a thing as I've heard of during the war, our colonel and our officers, down to the youngest subaltern, walked calmly up and down in the open, cheering us with words of encouragement and occasionally a drop from their own flasks. In fact, they were ready to do anything for us except to give us permission to smoke, and we knew that would have meant sentencing us to death.

Sergeants, corporals and lance corporals also oversaw the work, walking the open as fearlessly as the officers. The waves of shelling continued every half hour throughout the night for four or five minutes. When it was quiet, each man would continue cutting out a pit that would eventually be joined up with all the rest to create the new first line trench rumoured to be key to the largest attack made by the British Army to date.

If the record of 47th Division looms small in the story of Loos, then the record of Brigadier-General W. T. Thwaites has all but vanished. Within the overall fiasco of Loos, what sets Thwaites apart is found in the testimony of those who served under him. As soldier's soldier, when war broke out in August 1914, Lt-Col W. T. Thwaites, R. A., took over command of the 2nd London Division from Major-General C. C. Munro who moved on to command the First Army in France. Thwaites was responsible for the whole training of the Division both in England and in France until he was promoted to the rank of Brigadier-General 141st (5th London) on 2 June 1915. To avoid confusion with the 2nd Division, the 2nd London Division had already changed its name to 'London Division', changing again to 47th (London) Division under the command of Major-General C. St. L. Barter. The 141st (5/London) Brigade under Thwaites comprised 1/17th London (Poplar & Stepney), 1/18th London (London Irish), 1/19th London (St Pancras) and 1/20th London (Blackheath & Woolwich). From the start, Thwaites' men considered themselves better resourced than other units they came across. What was found wanting in men and munitions, he made up for in meticulous planning, attention to detail and above all, in training, which would result in both the immediate success of the assault at Loos at a cost of fewer casualties.

33. Brigadier-General W. T. Thwaites.

As one of Thwaites' men and proud to be so, Frank Edwards paraded as usual for drill one morning before the march to a piece of waste ground seven miles behind the lines. Marked out with tape and flags 'as if for athletics', as one observer put it, what this arena represented was every objective allotted to the 141st Infantry Brigade, with each trench and noticeable feature visible on the ground marked out as it would present itself on the day of the great push. To ensure that each man knew his part in the assault, these rehearsals were complete in every detail from the route taken through the complicated trench system recently dug, to the locations of munitions supplies and the evacuation of casualties. It was on this rehearsal field that the news was officially relayed to the men of the London Irish Rifles that they had been granted the honour of leading the charge. Laid out before them was the first cluster of flags representing the British trench system. A second row 700 yards away marked the line of the first German trench and 800 yards behind that the enemy's support trench. This second trench was the objective for the London Irish.

Unlike the British system, the German scheme of trench warfare saw the second trench more strongly fortified than the first, as the main position. It was therefore essential that the London Irish met their objective and captured it at the first rush. Each man was provided with a panorama sketch of his own front where the three attacking divisions opposite the villages of Hulluch and Loos were positioned. From left to right was the 1st, the 15th (Scottish) and the 47th (London). Higher up, opposite Hulluch and Haisnes the 9th (Scottish) Division, and looking to the Hohenzollern redoubt, a chalky earthwork that thrust out beyond the German front line trenches on rising ground, the 7th Division. North and south of the London Irish respectively would be the 19th (St Pancras) and 20th Battalion (Blackheath and Woolwich). The fourth unit comprising the 17th (Poplar and Stepney Rifles) would hold the original British front line as Brigade Reserve. The London Irish would make the initial advance in 'extended order' with four yards between every two men in order to make a less solid target than a massed shoulder to shoulder formation. Successive lines would go forward fifty yards apart. Once the second line had been taken, orders were to halt and let the other battalions pass. With the fifth line occupying the front German trench, as many lines following would take the enemy's third trench and as much ground as possible beyond it en route for the southern part of the Loos defences about 1,200 yards between the Bethune-Loos road and Loos cemetery at the south west corner of the village.

The first rehearsal revealed the value of Thwaites' initiative. All units waited between the rows of flags until the whistle sounded for the London Irish Rifles to leave their 'trench' for the charge forward. When they did so, it became immediately apparent that when carrying full kit, a rifle, 200 rounds of ammunition and a pick or shovel, it was not possible to cover as much as three quarters of a mile in one headlong charge. Instructions were then changed to have the men run the first fifty yards until clear of their own trenches where the enemy had a fixed target and known range for their shell fire. The attackers would then drop to a steady walk, finishing with a sprint for the last 100 yards into the German trench. Every day for a week, the men rehearsed not only the general attack but also what was known as the 'consolidation', where the captured German trenches would need to be reversed to face east as the new British front.

In a new departure from the previous assaults, the charge would be 'helped' with the use of poisonous gas. In this, the forward attackers would be 'protected' by smoke helmets, which were essentially hoods lined with canvas, large enough to cover the head. Tucked into the tunic collar, a rubber tube at the

34. In anticipation of a poison-gas attack.

mouth made it possible to breathe out but not in, while the canvas lining acted as a filter. The result, even on the training ground, was a hot, stuffy, suffocating experience made all the worse with the crude glass eyepieces constantly dropping out of alignment.

The time for retaliation had come, 'but not like for like', Belton Cobb recalled, believing that the German gas not only rendered men insensible, but if they recovered made them ill for the rest of their lives. Thanks to the efforts of the finely tuned propaganda machine, it was widely believed that the British formula was far more humane, causing only temporary unconsciousness. In the summer of 1915 *The War Illustrated* reported in great detail what it headlined 'The Horrors of the Poison War'. It declared the public to be well aware of the 'horrible savagery of the Germans in their use of poison-gas and asphyxiating shells', at the same time reminding readers that there remained much confusion on the subject. It noted that as was to be expected, the Germans were fighting foul, committing the 'most deadly crime' against Allied troops almost without the knowledge of the British public. Instead of employing 'a painless method of stupefying or slaughtering the allied troops', *The War Illustrated* explained, the enemy had experimented on tethered dogs to develop a long, lingering, agonising death lasting for days at a time.

In his book *The Poison War*, British scientist, A. A. Roberts, made it plain that from the very beginning of the war, allied troops had been 'systematically poisoned by the Germans in a manner publicly unknown'. After all, the German governing class 'had nothing left to guide it but the elemental brute instinct of self-preservation at any cost'. It had to be understood that the modern German was a new kind of savage of the most ferocious type, armed with scientific instruments of destruction, organised for slaughter by highly scientific means in his struggle for plunder and power. In a country remarkable for its chemical industries, Germany had been able to engineer a subtle and deadly form of poison attack on an unparalleled scale.

The War Illustrated claimed that the Germans had adapted regular bullets to contain a mixture of white and red phosphorus specifically designed to aggravate a wound, just four years after the signing of The Hague Convention. The same formula, also implanted into artillery shells, was a powerful irritant poison, giving off a noxious vapour that converted into highly toxic phosphoric acid on contact with the oxygen of the atmosphere. On entering the body, there was considerable difficulty getting the slightest wound to heal and only when the victim was recovering his strength did the phosphorus begin its evil work. Soldiers had left hospital outwardly fit and well only to be struck down with painful liver and kidney disorders, from which they might never recover. For months the surgeons were baffled until one French surgeon noticed that a slight wound to the arm of soldier shone in the dark and resulted in an agonising death seven days later. It was only after the discovery of these phosphorous munitions by French troops that 'the question of the German crime was definitely solved'. There *The War Illustrated* was prepared to let the matter rest, except to point out that if such things were allowed to continue, the result might be a war lasting many long and terrible years. Only when the legitimate use of asphyxiating gas was fully understood by 'everybody in the British Empire', could this urgent need to assist the troops come about.

Writing in 1916, Captain C.J.C. Street believed that the ultimate intention of the General Staff concerning the assault at Loos would not be revealed until long after the end of the war, 'if even then'. The general instructions as he knew them to be, were issued to the Fourth Corps, representing the southernmost portion of the First British Army. Here the line was held from the canal southward to the junction with the French. The objectives were Loos and Hill 70, the eastern slope of the valley behind the village where a position would be established to command Lens from the north. The French were to make a simultaneous attack from the direction of Souchez and then occupy the Vimy ridge to similarly threaten Lens from the south. In order to attain these objectives, a four-day bombardment of the enemy's position was to be undertaken, followed by an immediate assault on the fifth day. For half a

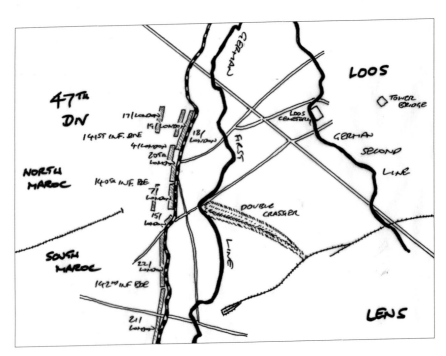

35. Map of battle positions, September 1915.

day throughout the rehearsal period everything would be quiet and then for five hours every gun in the district would concentrate on one section of the German line and its wire entanglement, with machine-gunners at the ready to halt any attempt to repair the damage. As the days passed so the bombardment became more frequent and more intense. Although aircraft observers reported the first two German trenches almost completely destroyed, they could not establish the condition of the dugouts cut deep into the chalk, most of which were sufficiently robust to survive the high explosives raining down on them. Frank Edwards was no more a cynic than any of his companions but he knew that the talk of a 'walk over' was at best optimistic.

The previous great 'experiments' in this war undertaken thus far at Neuve Chapelle, Ypres and Aubers Ridge had effectively squandered the 'old' British Army. But here on the fields of twentieth-century France a fantastical scenario was being played out on a level of destruction unequalled and only surpassed in its stupendous ineptitude. From previous encounters it had been learned that without exception, the first fifty yards of the initial assault would prove to be the most perilous should the enemy manage to restore their deadly machine-gun posts. It was common knowledge that the Germans dug deep, solidly and well. The most intensive artillery bombardment of the war thus far would only signal to the Germans to sit tight. When it came to an end they would re-establish themselves and take aim across the largest and most lethal range ever devised. At least that was the general expectation. So much so that Frank Edwards thought to refine the scenario, to give the Germans something else to think about before the howling line of hooded khaki figures bore down on them out of the gas cloud.

Chapter Six

On the Ball

Forty-eight hours before the Great Push, Frank Edwards found himself returned three miles behind the firing line from where he had been quartered during training. After handing in his overcoat and kit – except for his waterproof sheets, washing equipment and razor – to the Quartermaster's store, he was issued with two days' rations in addition to the usual iron ration. The pre-attack bombardment, comprising a huge number of gun positions dug in behind the lines, would see the infantry left to subsist on field rations while the supply wagons were used to ferry the extra artillery ammunition required. After taking his bayonet to the armourer to be sharpened, he was handed out either a pick or a shovel and fresh ammunition. Those men chosen as messengers, or for other specific purposes such as carrying wire cutters, were issued with coloured shoulder straps as distinguishing marks. At 21.00 hours on 24 September, Frank enjoyed a steak supper complete with an allowance of rum. At about 11.15 hours the whole battalion moved off to the trenches under the command of Lieutenant-Colonel J. P. Tredennick. At the entrance to the communication trenches Brigadier-General, later General Sir William Thwaites, KGB, was waiting. 'What a soldier he was!' Second Lieutenant S. F. Major recalled in his history of the 1st Battalion London Irish Rifles. One after another Thwaites took the officers by the hand with a cheery 'put it there, lad!' and a resounding 'Good luck!'.

'One had to serve under that General to realise what those words meant', S. F. Major affirmed in an echo of the same sentiment expressed by the nameless *Weekly Despatch* eyewitness. 'Heavens', the wounded warrior declared from his sickbed in London,

... you've got to be a soldier and to have been under fire and facing death for weeks to be able to understand what such words mean. No man can hear them

36. *The Weekly Despatch,*
31 October 1915.

and remain a coward, for you just feel that all the old people at home would scorn to receive you back unless you have done your utmost.

The Empire expected great things of the London Irish, chosen as they were to lead the whole division. 'I can't tell you the pride we felt,' the anonymous witness continued, remembering the few words uttered to the men by their commander, 'which stirred us to our inmost souls'.

Major-General William Thwaites may languish in the footnotes of First World War history, but he provides one of its finest leadership inspirations. While his professionalism is documented well enough in the history of the 47th Division, and to a degree his indomitable spirit, his name is missing from the histories of Loos along with the achievements of his 141st Brigade. He is more widely associated with the 46th Division, which has the distinction of being unique among those formations that would take part in the opening attack on the

Somme in July 1916 in not suffering its worst casualties of the war on that day. In the planning for the Somme, 46th Division was tasked with a diversionary attack against the German salient at Gommecourt to attract German reserves from further south where a British breakthrough was planned. However, the Division's perceived lack of offensive spirit was directly attributable to its ailing commander, and so the task of inspiring an offensive spirit and rebuilding confidence would pass to arguably the most successful field commander at Loos.

In all of the histories written about or referring to Loos, it is stated that the biggest artillery barrage in the war lasted four days before the attack on the morning of 25 September 1915. According to the eyewitness accounts drawn together by Second Lieutenant S. F. Major for his history of the 1st Battalion London Irish Rifles, however, the onslaught had begun almost a fortnight earlier. The same is indicated by the anonymous *Weekly Despatch* correspondent. Captain C. J. C. Street – in his capacity as a forward observation officer – makes no such observation, nor is there any indication in the official history, so we can only assume that the regular shelling of German lines was taken by the troops as an indication of the Big Push to come. Where all agree is that four days before the attack, the series of twelve-hour bombardments reached 'staggering proportions', although they were nowhere near as intense as they ought to have been due to a shortage of ammunition and the number of shells found to be faulty. As well as failing to cut the wire, these bombardments mostly served only to churn up the ground over which the infantry were expected to advance. Another observer, this time from a higher vantage point, was Rifleman C. Arthur who described an 'awe-inspiring sight' with the ground gradually sloping down towards the German front line and the village of Loos. Beyond it, silhouetted on the skyline was the pit winding gear tower dubbed by the Londoners 'Tower Bridge'. To its right loomed the vast black bulk of the Double Crassier.

Sleep was a rare event among the would-be attackers lining the trenches, their minds racked with the thoughts of what lay ahead and all the horrific possibilities of the coming dawn. Eventually, when the night was over and with the dawning of a weak early light, sets of bleary eyes were able to peer over the parapet towards the outlines of burning houses and broken church spires decorating the horizon beyond the German lines. Between them was No Man's Land, the ground where they would soon be making what for many would be their first and last dash, entirely unprotected and completely at the mercy of whatever fate decreed. The order was passed down the line to 'Stand to Arms'. The second order was to put on the smoke helmets. These unwieldy shrouds were initially hauled on with the lower part rolled back on the forehead, so that they could be pulled down and tucked into the collar in a matter of seconds. Seconds later, punctually at five o'clock, the first shell burst on the German lines resumed the bombardment. Three minutes later and the unutterable din was joined by the cacophony of German shells fired in answer. Shrapnel and high explosives burst all round the British trenches. Torn fragments of red hot iron whizzed in every direction. Here and there a direct hit into a trench decimated all it served to shelter. The *Weekly Despatch* eyewitness waited for the moment to experience the greatest adventure of his short life:

> As soon as we heard the great bombardment start we knew the big advance was going to begin. For nineteen solid days the guns banged away, 'till, as one wit in the regiment put it, it was a wonder the shells didn't bally well jam together in the air, so thick did they come over our heads.

Each artillery battery was allotted targets to be engaged at different periods over each of the four day bombardment prior to the attack. These were not specified, but described as days V, W, X, and Y. 'Throughout a breathless week we elaborated our plans, wrote Captain C. J. C. Street, 'each day bringing as a rule some modification of our original instructions.' So awesome an undertaking was it to move a battery of heavy guns that a Major with bitter experience of the task issued the prayer: 'O Lord, grant us victory in the coming struggle – but not in my sector.' Meanwhile, Street's daylight hours as Forward Observation Officer were spent peering out of slits, and the evenings measuring new angles and ranges on maps, until 'each one of us knew every stone in the country that lay in front of us by some pet name, and our maps developed strange diagrams in every possible combination of coloured chalks, for all the world like the diagram of the London Tubes.' In eager anticipation, the artillery detachments polished and oiled their guns over and over again. Men off duty stood about in groups, talking in hushed tones while the officers waited in the dugouts for the telephone to ring, announcing day V for 21 September.

Each phase of the action ahead had been long worked out to an empiric Zero, which was fixed for 5.50am on 25 September, the eagerly awaited Day Z. From the warning of 'Official time coming' when the watches were taken out in readiness, to the order of 'Hook your lanyards!' the gunners waited anxiously until the confirmation 'Time Zero!' and then 'Fire!' when every gun would be worked to its utmost capacity and every man sweating in the dust-laden pits, toiling as never before to feed them, pouring shell after shell into the enemy trenches in 'such a blasting hurricane of fire' writes Captain Street. 'The resistance prepared for our attack shall wither away in its deadly breath', he hoped. When the call eventually came for battery action, strings of orders began to pour in from the section commanders that were echoed by the Number One and then the senior subaltern calling for 'report battery ready to fire!' A long, interminable minute later and the faint buzz of the telephone gave way to the order to 'Fire No. 1 gun!' and the Battle of Loos had begun.

37. An artillery forward observation officer, 'the brain centre of Britain's Big Guns'.

The anticipation rapidly gave way to routine, with teams of men relieving each other in the hot and dusty gun emplacements. Officers would call on section commanders to take over the notebook, pencil and megaphone to carry on 'the ceaseless clamour … the periodic roaring, as of a thunderstorm controlled by an angel with a stop-watch'. Eventually the deafening intermittent cacophony took on

> … a strangely soothing affect on the senses. First one loses the din of the surrounding batteries, then fails to notice the report of one's own guns a few feet away, giving orders mechanically notwithstanding. Perhaps a stifled yawn and a glance at the watch – is that infernal fellow never coming to relieve me? Then the warning voice of the telephonist, 'Fresh target coming through, sir!' and the wandering attention leaps into watchfulness again.

Forward observation officers such as Street watched the black and yellow smoke clouds of the bursting high explosive, or the cotton wool-like puffs of the shrapnel either hit or fall short of their targets until a particular section of trench practically disappeared, leaving only a white scar.

A fascinating business this on so fine an autumn day, so fascinating that all sense of time is lost, all conjecture as to whether the enemy will take it into his head to select our observation post as a target is forgotten. The only thing in the world is the measured fall of the shell and the swift framing of the consequent order, the only pleasure the deep satisfaction of a well-placed round, the only despair the haunting memory of a shot wasted that might have been saved by a different procedure.

On the whole, the material effect of such a bombardment was hard to judge. Despite what Captain Street calls the 'high science of modern gunnery', the percentage of direct hits was comparatively small. Nevertheless, the four long days of ceaseless bombardment from early morning until it became too dark to observe the fall of the rounds never allowed the enemy a moment's respite.

While the batteries busied themselves replenishing ammunition and overhauling equipment, at least one gun per battery fired steadily throughout the hours of darkness onto the German billets and at places where reinforcements had to pass on their way to the firing line. These few rounds per hour were deemed sufficient to keep men huddled in cellars with little or no possibility of sleep. As Captain Street observed, 'the moral effect upon troops already shaken by bombardment is enormous, as we ourselves have had bitter cause to know in the earlier months of the war.' Quoting from the diary of a private in the Second Reserve Infantry Regiment (Prussian), which later fell into British hands, Street records that on 21 September:

Towards mid-day the trenches had already fallen in many places. Dug-outs were completely overwhelmed ... most of them fled, leaving rifles and ammunition behind ... the air was becoming heated from so many explosions.

On the 22nd:

Shells and shrapnel are bursting all round ... in places where the trench had disappeared I crawled on my hands and knees amid a hail of bullets.

On the 23rd he wrote:

Our look-out post was completely destroyed, and my comrades killed in it ... even the strongest man may lose his brain and nerves in a time like this.

And on the 24th:

The fourth day of this terrible bombardment ... I am sorry to say that there is no reply from our artillery.

Other prisoners on being interrogated testified to the awful effects of the bombardment. One in particular, an artillery officer, carried an order that revealed what Street described as 'the secret of the ineffectiveness of the enemy's reply', which indicates that it was not only the British gunners who were short on big guns and ammunition. After a brief analysis setting out the measures to be taken in case of a British offensive, the order stated that the Allies probably enjoyed the advantage of a two-to-one ratio of artillery in this sector. While mentioning nothing about a lack of shells, it directed that the fire on British targets should be confined to the most important and those that the gunners stood the best chance of hitting. While the British were seemingly prepared to indulge in an explosive orgy of indiscriminate artillery fire, under no circumstances were the German battery commanders allowed to be drawn into anything approaching what the order described as 'an artillery duel'.

The advanced trench where 1st Battalion London Irish Rifles squatted in anticipation of the attack contained the dreaded gas cylinders and the engineers to work them. Those attacking units comprising the second and third lines spent the night in the assembly trench, while the fourth line platoon occupied the old fire trench. It would be their job to move forward at the last moment along a communication trench when the other lines had started out. They would then rush into the assembly trench, climb over the parapet and go forward. The final burst of the bombardment would be the cue for the greatest advance yet seen on the Western Front.

Until the light failed, Captain Street and his fellow gunners had been busily shelling the Double Grassier, believed to be alive with machine-gun emplacements. Street had been in his observation post for most of the day and able to walk in safety to and from his observation point all hours through country lined with artillery batteries. At about seven o'clock, however, things began to change. Enemy shells began bursting all around him. As soon as he started his walk homewards along the Harrow Road, he noticed that several houses had been destroyed since the morning and the roads had become peppered with shell-holes. There were no casualties but the route was effectively obstructed.

Street eventually reached his battery to discover that orders had been received to be ready to move out at the shortest possible notice, in case of a general advance the following day. Although they were prepared for this eventuality, this was the official pronouncement of what Street viewed as 'the decisive struggle, the Waterloo of the campaign at last!' Far from the Allied plan being known to all but a handful of the Top Brass, Captain Street recalls that the 'glorious prospect of a scrap' had long been in the air. Spirits rose accordingly and little by little as the secret decisions and plans made by the strategists percolated down. Street felt that too much had been allowed to be known from the start, with documents detailing the proposed operations circulated in some cases as much as a fortnight before the selected day. In the field, moreover, it was impossible to prevent details becoming common knowledge within an 'incredibly short time'. It was, Street felt, 'practically equivalent to sending the originals across to the enemy with one's compliments'.

He claimed that the examination of prisoners showed that the German general staff had full knowledge of Allied plans many days before the planned attack and had made all the necessary arrangements to meet it. One captured document even contained a map showing the position of every Allied battery with only two exceptions in the whole of Street's own sector. 'It seems fairly certain that this was due to the most efficient espionage and not to aerial observation' he concluded. There is little doubt that through their spies and general observation the Germans knew pretty much the exact nature of the planned attack on Loos. The sustained burst of reciprocal shelling was designed to rattle the nerves of the attackers ready and waiting for the signal to go over the top. So small were the odds of avoiding injury or death that the fear of both gave way to relief with each exploding shell or fragment of shrapnel passing harmlessly by. Ten minutes before the whistle was due to blow, the order was passed down the line to fix bayonets. Above the heads of the London Irish, sandbags spat and exploded from the smack of heavy calibre machine-gun fire.

★ ★ ★

Philip Gibbs, watching the preliminary bombardment from atop a black slagheap beyond Noeux-les-Mines, later pieced together much of the story of the main battle from accounts of officers who had survived and from men in different parts of the field. The *Weekly Despatch* relied on a remarkably detailed and comprehensive overview from its single source. Whereas the wounded warrior claimed to have witnessed first hand much of the initial offensive, Gibbs observed that 'no man could see more than his immediate neighbourhood'. The value of the *Despatch* account is in its echoes of other eyewitness accounts that went otherwise unrecorded. In his influential post-war book, *Realities of War*, Gibbs skilfully deals with the strange incidents brought about by the euphoria of war, when men's spirits are 'uplifted by that mingling of exultation and fear which is heroism, and with queer episodes almost verging on comedy in the midst of death and agony, at the end of a day of victory, most ghastly failure.'

Approaching Zero Hour, the artillery went silent except for the odd shell falling on the German trenches, which was meant to deceive the enemy into a false sense of security. 'Storms of gunfire broke loose from our batteries a week before the battle,' wrote Gibbs.

The weather was heavy with mist and a drizzle of rain. Banks of smoke made a pall over all the arena of war, and it was stabbed and torn by the incessant flash of bursting shells. I stood on the slagheap, staring at this curtain of smoke, hour after hour, dazed by the tumult of noise and by that impenetrable veil which hid all human drama.

An officer at his side found it all very boring. There was not 'a damn thing to be seen' he complained. Another officer was convinced that the attack would be, as the generals suggested, a walkover and with any living German by now reduced to 'a gibbering idiot with shell-shock'. The first officer was unconvinced, imagining the Germans playing cards in their deep dugouts, indifferent to even the highest explosives raining down on them. 'It's stupendous, all the same' he reckoned, awestruck by the mighty pounding; 'By God! Hark at that! It seems more than human. It's like some convulsion of nature.' There was no adventure in modern war, sighed the bored officer. It had been reduced to 'a dirty scientific business, engineered by chemists and explosive experts'.

'Our men will have adventure enough when they go over the top at dawn,' the other officer answered, concluding that 'hell must be a game compared with that.' At 05.30 hours on the morning of 25 September 1915, the wind was slowing and shifting southwards with only a slight possibility of improvement. The conditions were not ideal for the deployment of the 'new weapon', but the British generals remained determined to give the enemy 'a touch of their own little game'. 'God knows how we had clamoured for it', admitted the *Weekly Despatch* narrator, rueful of the pitiless use of the new horror by the Germans against the defenceless Canadians and others at Givenchy.

At 05.50 hours the experts agreed that there was sufficient wind to send the lethal cloud of gas rolling across No Man's Land towards the enemy trenches. The taps were turned on the 5,243 mysterious cylinders labelled 'stout' that had been stored in numbered positions along the line. It had not been a popular fatigue carrying each one of these unwieldy items along the line slung on a pole, one cylinder to two men. Each weighing 200lbs, they wobbled about violently and 'were unpleasantly heavy'. Even had the going been good, it would have been as 'easy as walking a greasy pole', but the multitude of angles and corners along the length of the trench system 'had tested the last resources in battalion expletives', S. F. Major confided. Their eventual use into a slight westerly wind, with just a suggestion of south in it, released 150 tons of poisonous gas rolling across No Man's Land towards the German lines, much to the relief of Major General C. H. Foulkes, who organised the Special Gas Service.

Foulkes recalls in his book, entitled *Gas*, his standing atop of a tall wooden tower that had been specifically constructed as an observation post. From there he was able to witness the awe-inspiring spectacle. The first release of the pungent substance comprised a thick, dense 50-foot high noxious veil shifting forward almost imperceptibly. 'The whole countryside to the front for as far as the eye could see was enveloped in what appeared to be a vast prairie conflagration.' The British guns were by now answered by enemy artillery. High explosive shells crashed into the trenches and shrapnel screamed overhead. Throughout the whole of the four days' bombardment along the whole of the British front, the enemy had not reinforced any particular sector, but instead had kept their reserves in a state of immediate readiness at various railway centres. Captain Street considered it very probable that during 23 and 24 September, fresh batteries were placed in position between Vendin-le-Vieil and Lens, and that it was these that came into action on the afternoon and evening of the 24th. His supposition would be borne out by the enemy's ability to bring about 'a terrific fire' on Loos as soon as the British troops entered it.

'The din was ear-splitting' explains Second Lieutenant S. F. Major in his regimental history. 'It was well for us that our trenches at this point were deep and of the best London Irish manufacture!' With remarkably few casualties at that stage, the men stood to arms in the trenches as billows of white, yellow, brick red and black smoke rose sixty to eighty feet above the plain, 'very different from our practice attacks on those trenches in the sunshine behind the lines!' Beyond this deadly fog was the first objective, the enemy's front line; the strongly fortified Valley Cross Roads, commanding the way to Loos. At 06.00 hours, as flashes of shrapnel bursts rocked and quivered the hanging clouds, the attackers received final instructions. In looking to their rifles, bayonets, and gas masks, the bombers tied to their left sleeves the brassards to be used for igniting the ball bombs they carried. Towards zero hour the German shelling became wild and patchy. Scaling ladders were fixed against the trench sides ready for the assault. By 06.15 hours the infantry fire had slackened appreciably. A Scottish officer later told Philip Gibbs that he had asked an English counterpart how the gas was going. The English officer looked about him anxiously with a wetted finger held up to get the direction of the wind and replied that it was going fine. Then the slow progress of the gas cloud stalled half way across No Man's Land. A swirl of wind changed its course, blew it down a gully and swept it right into the narrow trenches sheltering men of the Black Watch laden down with their spades, bombs and sandbags, waiting. 'A queer kind o' stink!' exclaimed one of them, sniffing the air before he and some of the men began coughing. Others were rubbing their eyes. Unlike the initial attacking troops who were equipped with crude gas hoods as protection, from what Gibbs was told these Royal Highlanders had nothing.

Geoffrey Belton Cobb in his disguised account of the fictional Eatonshires reported the same 'bitter tang in the air'. High above the British trenches palls of smoke and gas were rising every few yards. The grey-yellow columns, narrow at the bottom where they left the cylinders, spread out as they rose until they were caught by the wind towards the German lines, spreading out into a large blanket. Meanwhile a number of engineers working on the cylinders were overcome with the backlash of their new weapon, falling down and themselves gasping and choking. Although German shellfire was pounding into their position, the effect of the gas was far worse. Brave men who had been keeping it together despite the murderous artillery barrage were now experiencing a new kind of terror that left them helplessly coughing and spitting blood as the chlorine did what it was designed to do. Dozens of men fell and died. Others lay helpless, frothing at the mouth with lips turned scarlet, their bodies racked with pain and bouts of tearing nausea. Many would suffer an unspeakably painful lingering death, wafting in air fouled with the stench of deadly chemicals that filled the mouth and flooded the lungs as though drowning on dry land. For those survivors eventually ordered into battle they would do so with heads racked with pain, fighting off a terrific thirst that could not be quenched, for to drink water after inhaling the lethal cocktail meant instant death. Those left behind would wait for their lungs to erupt, then mix with a greenish froth from the stomach, and only when the colour of the skin turned from a pallid white to a greenish yellow and then to black, and the eyes assumed a glassy stare, did insensibility finally turn to death.

Unaware of such horror awaiting him, Frank Edwards held himself ready to spring into action, crouched with five or six others by one of the ten assault ladders designated to each platoon. All along the trench the *Weekly Despatch*'s nameless narrator witnessed men 'tightening a buckle here and a strap there … everybody was in the best of spirits'. In fact, he believed they had never felt keener for the fray:

> It seemed as if at last the war for us had really begun. Some looked a trifle pale, others were extra jolly, but all had a look of determination different from any expression they usually wore.

Indeed, even at a moment of such tension there were those who found time for a joke, obliging a sergeant in his wish for a 'Blighty One' – an injury severe enough to get out of the trenches and be sent home honourably but without permanent damage. The sergeant gleefully exclaimed that he had been wounded, only to discover that it was warm muddy water running down his face from the lump of clay hurled at his head and not blood. Minutes later, that same sergeant would be seen taking on fourteen Germans defending a communications trench. Major Beresford, the officer in command, then gave the signal.

Sergeant Sadler was about to go over the top when he was told in no uncertain terms to get down. Seconds later and the parapet above his head

erupted from the spiteful spatter of machine-gun fire showering the waiting men with exploding earth and shards of chalk. His own head cowered,
Second Lieutenant S. F. Major then witnessed a sight 'that might have made
the author of the phrase about the contemptible British Army open his eyes
in wonderment'. The *Weekly Despatch* correspondent reported likewise that
one set of men – 'footballers by profession' – had resolved to take a football
along with them. On discovery of their plan, they were ordered to leave it
back at base, but

> ... these old members of the London Irish Football Club were not to be done
> out of the greatest game of their lives – the last to some of them, poor fellows.
> And so it was that just before the signal, the leather turned up again mysteriously.

S. F. Major reported more precisely that it was rifleman Frank Edwards who
was spotted 'calmly using valuable breath to blow up a football as though
the matter in hand were going to be a cup-tie!' Major confirmed that it was
Edwards who

> ... had conceived the great idea of dribbling the ball into the enemy's lines. He
> had cherished the notion for some time. It was discussed freely but frowned upon
> by authority, which gave the platoon officer no choice other than to order the
> ball to be deflated.

'Not that he was windy', added Edwards in a later BBC wireless interview,

> He was the bravest of all and the youngest, being only 18, I believe. He thought it
> would be exposing ourselves to more risk and he knew what we had coming to
> us in the morning.

Edwards told listeners that he had made sure that another ball was kept ready.
Whatever might happen in the battle, the sight of British soldiers coolly passing the ball from one to another would give the enemy their biggest shock of
the war. In writing the history of the 1st Battalion London Irish Rifles, Major
explained how the idea continued to fascinate Edwards and it was he who was
determined to go through with it, whatever the consequences. Having taken
the ball out of his haversack and blown it up, he managed to get it laced up
just before the great guns to the rear of the British lines lifted their barrels for
the assault on the German second line, putting the enemy into disarray it was
thought, and assisting the initial progress of the advancing troops. Hopefully
the enemy would have barely begun setting up new positions before the attackers were upon them. But the time for such debate and supposition was over.

'It was like hell let loose, especially when "Jerry" replied with high explosives' Edwards recalled. 'It was impossible to hear even shouted orders.'

★ ★ ★

At forty minutes past zero, or 6.30am, every battery lifted its fire from the enemy front line to the second. In the dull, grey light at 5.30am until the moment the assault began, Captain Street was hardly able to see further than the front line trenches from his observation post. 'The expectancy of viewing the greatest battle in history was to our little party in the O.P. strangely banal,' he recalls.

> I, for one, could not grasp the reality of it; I felt as though I were in a box waiting for the actors to come upon a stage before which the curtain had risen prematurely. There was no sign of battle, no movement that the eye could detect over the whole of the wide prospect before us. And then suddenly came time zero, bringing with it a scene that could never be forgotten. From the whole length of our front trench, as far as the eye could reach, rose vertically at first, a grey cloud of smoke and gas, which, impelled by a gentle wind, spread slowly towards the enemy's trenches, very soon enveloping the whole of our range of vision in its opaque veil. This was our view of the assault, this dismal vapour the aura that was to surround a thousand sacrifices, the cloak that was to hide a thousand gallant deeds, the winding-sheet that was to enwrap so many a hero.

While the British batteries fired on the German second line, an army of dummies worked by strings operated by the 21st and 22nd Londons appeared to the right of the attacking 18th. In the smoke and confusion they were realistic enough to draw enemy fire from the real attackers who from the German perspective were in outward appearance

> … hardly more human than the dummies further south – strange figures, hung about with sandbags and bandoliers of ammunition, with no caps, but smoke-helmets on their heads rolled into a sort of turban, with the mouth piece nodding by way of ornament over their foreheads.

Alan Maude, editor of the history of the 47th Division, relates that the 141st Brigade had the furthest to go. Their objective was the German second line on the Bethune-Lens Road where they would join the 6th Battalion to Loos cemetery. Two battalions, the 20th to the right and 19th to the left would continue on once the primary objective had been met by the 1/18th London Irish Rifles. 'We passed the word along by signs', Edwards later told BBC listeners. 'A minute to go, and then it was "London Irish Lead On!"' But the order could not be heard all along the line in the noise of the shelling. Each man momentarily looked to others for a signal to climb the ladders and out into the lethal hail of high velocity bullets. 'Over you go, lads' came the call, leading the entire line to spring up as one, 'some with a prayer, not a few making the sign of the Cross.' Over the parapet and with his heart pounding, Edwards lobbed the ball ahead, 'just as a goalkeeper might fling it back up the field'.

All Captain Street was able to witness from the columns scaling the ladders and starting to double across the open ground were those seeming to trip as they ran. At first he thought that the British wire had not been thoroughly cut and that these men had become entangled in some loose strands. But it soon it became all too clear that these were men being torn down in their droves by the waves of enemy machine-gun fire. Edwards' fellow football enthusiasts, riflemen Micky Mileham, Bill Taylor and Jimmy Dalby, had spread out like a line of forwards going after the ball.

A hefty kick came off the boot of Mileham who then passed it to Dalby and on to Taylor. All the while shells burst among them and shrapnel ripped through the stinking air. S. F. Major recalled how the men passed and re-passed the ball until they disappeared in a smoke cloud with the ball still being punted towards the German front line. The unwieldy smoke hoods did not help. 'To our horror', recalled Major, 'the wind changed again slightly'. Gas and smoke came drifting back, causing the crude gas helmets to be immediately pulled on and tucked into collars.

Many men, slow in adjusting their masks, fell choking to the ground. 'One fellow thought that smoking a pipe would keep the gas away: he puffed away furiously – but *he* was soon out!' In a letter home, Sergeant Sydney Sadler cursed the inadequate headgear they were forced to wear, as well as the lack of steel helmets. Rifleman Arthur remembered there being very little wind when the gas was eventually released, that the gas hung about in a bank only a few yards in front of the trenches so that that when he went over the top the men soon passed through it and into the clear air beyond. S. F. Major recalls that although the gas had been turned off, the noxious veil hung like a cloud in No Man's Land, making it impossible to see more than fifty yards ahead.

South of the charging Londoners, Philip Gibbs describes the French troops waiting for their own attack to take place. They cheered the men of the London Irish as they went forward, with cries of '*Vivent les Anglais!*' and '*A mort-les Boches!*' Seeing one man kicking a football in advance of the others, they shouted 'He is mad!' 'The poor boy is a lunatic!' screamed one shocked observer. 'He is not mad' said a French officer who had lived in England. 'It is a *Beau Geste*. He is a sportsman scornful of death. That is the British sport.' In his record for the *Weekly Despatch* the wounded eyewitness reported the footballers going after the ball 'just as cool as if on the field, passing it from one to the other, though

38. Edwards's Ball.

39. Loos. 'Hi Ref! blow up, he's off-side' – Harry Tyers.

40. Calling the men together.
(Ruth Cobb)

the bullets were flying thick as hail. They cried out "On the ball, London Irish", just as they might have done at Forest Hill.' Captain W. M. Escombe of the 1/20 London Regiment recalls the moment when he glanced over the top to see in the dense smoke

> ... the Irish advancing in line. Weird and uncanny they look – mere shadows in the curling yellow fog – but they never hesitate; each line adjusts itself and disappears. Here indeed is borne the fruit of all that training at Hatfield, St Albans, and in our days of 'rest' behind the line; for nothing but the absolute habit of moving in line at five paces interval could enable men to do so under these hellish conditions.

Major Beresford, who was second in command, went down badly wounded. Another officer named Hamilton was also wounded and had to be placed under arrest to prevent him going on. A sergeant (unnamed) was burnt to death by a petrol bomb. Major General Foulkes from atop the tall observation tower witnessed the 1/18th dribbling the football in front of them as the wind changed direction, blowing his smoke and gas barrage back into them. There were ominous gaps in the line of the 1st Division as those Scots that were able, cursing and groaning from the effects of the gas, went over the top with handkerchiefs tied about their choking mouths and noses. In No Man's Land many of them fell in the sweep of machine-gun fire and exploding shrapnel. While the Highlanders went forward with their pipes, two brigades of the Londoners on their right were advancing in the direction of the long, double slag heap south west of Loos. Some of them were blowing mouth organs, playing the music-hall song 'Hullo, hullo, it's a different girl again!' and the 'Robert E. Lee', until one musician after another fell in a crumpled heap with shrapnel bursting over them from shells ploughing deep into the ground and sending up great scoops of earth and steel fragments. Maude records each line moving forward at a quick pace, 'evidence' he pronounced, 'of the rehearsal, in that despite the smoke there was no deviation of the line taken'.

The British guns blasted away 'like ten thousand thunderstorms' over the heads of the attackers, sporting their weird respirators. Between the waves of gas and the blinding smoke filling the 400-yard space between the opposing trenches, some cover was provided for a few of the attackers while others, including Frank Edwards, were half-asphyxiated. With 'every step taken with regimental precision' Patrick MacGill records in his book *The Great Push*, only to the right was there some confusion and irregularity as though the men were wavering. 'No fear!' he quickly established, 'The boys on the right were dribbling the elusive football towards the German trench.' The vicious barbed wire, otherwise impenetrable, had been smashed to smithereens by the unrelenting shower of British shells, allowing the attackers through. Recalling his own experience of the 'mad footballers', the *Weekly Despatch* correspondent believed that they actually kicked the ball 'right into the enemy's trench with the cry, "Goal!" though not before some of them had been picked off on the way'.

'It was a London Irishman dribbling a football toward the goal', wrote Gibbs, 'and he held it for fourteen hundred yards – the best-kicked goal in history.' But soon, as Edwards later explained, 'all thoughts of the ball had gone', as choking and heaving, they tried to secure their unwieldy gas hoods.

> They weren't much use. In fact, I felt worse with mine on than off. We captured the first trench and then carried on towards the second – at least, those who were left did. I went down with a bullet through the thigh and hand and took no further part in the attack ... As for the ball, that went with some of the footballers – to eternity – where they will still be playing the game, as they always did in the old 1st Battalion of the London Irish.

Frank had felt a sharp pain through his thigh and hand as though he had been pierced with a hot wire. At the same moment he felt weak and giddy. His rifle

41. The London volunteers take their objective.

dropped. He felt his knees give way and he fell to the ground. After the first feeling of faintness he did not lose consciousness but felt sick, and the burning sensation in his thigh left his leg limp and numb. He made a point of noting the heroism of his comrade Micky Mileham during his BBC broadcast:

> If he is still alive, I hope he is listening tonight. He used my field dressing on my leg and put on a tourniquet, which probably stopped me from bleeding to death, and he used his own dressing on my hand. It was broad daylight by this time, and one of the enemy machine-gunners got us spotted. All the time Micky was doing me up the bullets were spattering round us, turning up the soil as they buried themselves in the ground.

Both men had started to develop a nasty cough. Their voices turned husky from the inhalation of the poisonous gas. Their skin took on the same yellow tinge as that covering the faces of those less fortunate scattered all around them. Provided he could make it back to the dressing station, Frank's wounds meant a ticket back home. But while the machine-gun posts were gradually taken, there still lurked German snipers.

> Just as Micky had finished dressing my wounds, he rolled over with a bullet in his chest. I could do nothing for him. I can remember him saying 'I'm all right, Eddie.' Then we both shouted for help, and eventually some of the boys got us

into the trench. What happened after is very vague. I found myself on the 29th en route for 'Blighty.' If ever a chap deserved the D.C.M. Micky did.

Frank's thoughts then returned to the carnage about him. For some of the London Irish who kicked and passed the ball it was the ultimate game of their lives. The ball continued in play before the line of charging, eerie hooded shapes disappeared through the drifting, poisonous fog. Following up the assault, stretcher-bearer MacGill did what he could for the dying and the sorely wounded, 'lives maimed and finished ... all the romance and roving that makes up the life of a soldier gone forever'. Against one of the tangled webs of barbed wire he came across 'a limp lump of pliable leather, the football which the boys had kicked across the field'.

★ ★ ★

Four days after the initial attack, S. F. Major wondered who amongst the wave of exhausted attackers could ever forget the morning General Thwaites rode amongst them on horseback like a latter day medieval king, nonchalantly cantering to and fro, having jumped the trenches and barbed wire defences, defying the shrapnel in an authentic display of the modern pentathlon: 'A soldier indeed!' the bomber declared. The commander of the 141st Brigade announced:

> Not only am I proud to have had the honour of being in command of such a regiment as yours ... for I can tell you that it was the London Irish who helped to save a whole British Army Corps. You've done one of the greatest actions of the war.

Based on the success of the initial assault by IV Corps, Lieutenant-General Sir Henry Rawlinson had requested in a telephone call that XI Corps be moved up at once. In his comprehensive review of the battle, *Loos 1915*, Nick Lloyd states that Rawlinson was 'obviously anxious to exploit the great success of the 15th Division'. He had been told that he need keep nothing in reserve and that immediately following success another corps would be pushed through. It was on this understanding that General Sir Douglas Haig sent word to make sure that XI Corps was ready to advance, only to discover that the plans agreed upon with Sir John French were, like the reserves, not in place. As for the efforts of the 47th Division, General Thwaites genuinely imagined that 'the whole Empire will be proud whenever in after years the battle of Loos comes to be written.'

As the lead attackers, the men of the 1st Battalion London Irish Rifles were the first to experience the effects of charging through poison gas. Many felt the full effects of its potency, ripping off the cumbersome masks before reaching the German front line, yelling their war-cry 'Hurroo!' as they leapt over, making for their second line objective. The nameless survivor recalling the events to readers of the *Weekly Despatch* explained how impossible it was to describe a charge to anyone who had not experienced it. 'You can only feel it' he suggested, asking the uninitiated to imagine running down London's Oxford Street with people at every window each raining down half a dozen bricks. 'A kind of madness that comes over a man as he thrusts a bayonet into another, hearing the shriek as the steel goes through him.' It was so unimaginable that the Loos survivor gave it up, turning his thoughts instead to the voice of the 'dear old chaplain' – the Padre, who made the charge with them, giving his blessing and absolution to the men as they fell on every side. Patrick MacGill also paid tribute to Father Fox-Lane. In *The Great Push* he vividly describes him going over with the men and showing great courage under fire.

'Every bomber is a hero,' the recovering rifleman added, grateful for the numbers of defenders cleared by them, 'for he has to rush on fully exposed, laden with enough stuff to send him to Kingdom Come if a chance shot or a stumble sets him off.' Second Lieutenant S. F. Major was in charge of a bomber platoon. Besides his rifle and grenades he carried packs of clumsy looking tubular missiles packed into metal containers worn across his chest, known as Battye bombs – rough iron castings the shape and size of a glass tumbler with oblong lozenges cut into the sides so as to fragment on detonation. A plug of hard wood with a hole drilled through it contained a detonator rammed into the mouth of the device above an ammonal blasting charge. A crude lighter comprising two cardboard 'thimbles', one inside the other, ignited the fuse by pressing down the outer thimble and twisting out the inner one, which then lit the three to five second fuse. Unreliable in the extreme, these devices were either useless in wet weather or, as they proved to be at Loos, were responsible for killing more bombers than their intended victims.

According to the official history of the 47th Division the perilous advance of the London Territorials was 'easy going' with the second German line reached well on time. Although it was still strongly wired, it was less well defended than thought. The real difficulties began with the German first line taken on by the other regiments as the initial attackers stormed off to take the village of Loos itself. Sergeant Sadler at first found his initial journey across No Man's Land and into the German lines less hazardous than he feared, with the pylons of 'London Bridge' acting as the guide to his target of Loos cemetery 2,000 yards away. 'But in the mist,' he added, 'everything became hidden and we had to wander on. Behind us, we were aware of the casualties on both sides.' All the while 'the stabbing and shooting and bombing continuing until the men were fit to drop'. Concealed Maxims – snipers with telescopic sights and unlimited supplies of food and ammunition – continued firing away until they were themselves picked off.

The most macabre episode was the struggle to take the cemetery, which had been transformed into a makeshift fort with great tombstones, crosses and pillars placed one on top of the other. Here savage hand-to-hand fighting took place and where 'it seemed for all the world as if the living could not supply sufficient food for the slaughter and the dead were rising again to die once more.' There was little room for such sentiment at the time. The cemetery was cleared and the assault moved on. S. F. Major recalled the Scots who went racing through the village yelling their war-cry, 'Ninth of May, you B–s!' referring to the attack on Aubers Ridge where captured fellow countrymen were said to have been stripped of their kilts, driven across No-Man's Land and exterminated with machine-gun fire. Major remembered too how Germans occupying fortified houses in the village at Valley Cross Roads held up one wave of attack. On the order of 'Bombers Up!' Major and his men doubled forward, and standing in line hurled their bombs through gaping shell holes in the walls and roofs of the shattered houses leaving 41 enemy dead before sweeping on to take the final objective.

The notorious Hill 70, *Weekly Despatch* readers learned, was some five or six miles across and was hardly a hill as such. In fact, so flat was it that it was quite possible for both German and British troops to be occupying it simultaneously without even realising they were on a hill at all. The London Irish went clean over it in the first rush, beyond Loos in the direction of Lens, which they had hoped to capture. The Germans, however, brought up reinforcements to prevent the loss of Lens and the road to Douai. Concentrating the whole of their counter-attack upon the unseasoned troops who had only a fortnight's experience at the front, the enemy looked to exploit the situation laid out before them. The plan almost worked, at one point nearly losing the British all of their hard-won gains. However, large quantities of supplies had been moved up into the German's former third line of trenches, which now formed the British first line with much of the sandbag parapets shifted to the other side before the counter-attack opened up.

'Stick to it, lads' urged one of the London Irish officers, reiterating the call that everything depended on them. From his hospital bed in London the anonymous *Weekly Despatch* witness told of how General Thwaites' rousing words had come back to each man: 'Remember you're Irish and the Empire expects great things of you' – even though very few of the men were actually Irish. Deeply heartened by this stirring, if flawed, pronouncement, the commentator claimed that there would be no giving in. According to this same source, advancing Germans soldiers yelled out the threat of Von Hindenburg coming with half-a-million men, which was greeted with an equally stout 'Begorra!' when it became the turn of the London Irish to mow down the oncoming waves of charging men. Those stretches of barbed wire destroyed by their own guns, now offered the new defenders little or no protection as the Germans came on. So sufficient was the required firepower metered out that the rifles threatened to burn the very hands that held them.

The men of the London Irish were at this point a long way from their own lines, isolated and alone. 'The strain on the nerves was something terrific' the vibrant *Weekly Despatch* account continued. All the while close pals and comrades were 'pipped in the head by a bullet, or in the body by a piece of shrapnel, their dying thoughts no doubt far away among the green hills of old Ireland'. As another eyewitness less flamboyantly put it, the 1st Division was checked. 'We caught it badly' Philip Gibbs was later told. Bloodied and plastered in wet chalk, gassed men gasped for air fouled by the fumes and dust from artillery fire and the gas and smoke of 11,000 candles and 25,000 phosphorus hand-grenades; 10,000 bombs from 29 4-inch Stoke mortars, thousands more from 135 catapults; 95mm and 2-inch trench-mortars were enveloping the enemy artillery observers and machine-gunners in an impenetrable cloud.

Sir Douglas Haig, on instruction from Sir John French, had prepared the attack plan on the basis that two divisions of reserve troops would be at his disposal within two or three hours of the initial attack to reinforce or exploit success. According to Henry Williamson:

> Th reserves which the First Army commander fighting the battle had requested, again and again, to be two thousand yards behind the British front line, were then six miles back, and in no fit condition to march on until they had rested. They had been kept back deliberately by Field-Marshal Sir John French.

Williamson clearly had little time for the 63-year-old British commander, he observed,

> His body was heavy on its frame with abdominal muscles sagging from desk-work, not from indulgence in food. He had reached the time of life when a man reflects rather than acts; and for over a year of war he had been continually frustrated. He had lived with grief: the flower of his army had been destroyed. Anxiety gnawed him, a fox under his cloak.

While opinion about the military leadership in the First World War has shifted back and forth somewhat since Alan Clark's 1960s indictment, Sir John French was economical with the truth in his ninth Despatch to General Headquarters, dealing in part with the Battle of Loos. Haig demanded it should be corrected with regard to the question of the deployment of reserves, the matter over which French was eventually sacked.

42. Sir John French.

For those who paid the ultimate price, the whole of the third day of fighting passed without relief. 'We could hardly stand from fatigue', the *Weekly Despatch* eyewitness continued in his steadfast, uncomplaining manner, having been in action since Saturday morning. 'Fight on, lads' cried an officer minutes before he was killed. 'The division looks to you' he reminded his exhausted men. 'This is bound to end sooner or later. Let it be in a way that will never be forgotten when they hear of it at home in London and Ireland.'

Henry Williamson's alter-ego, Phillip Maddison, is at this point a chemical corporal. He comes into contact with the acting commanding officer of one of the supporting battalions, a testy, domineering character known – because of his unwholesome, cadaverous image – as 'Spectre' West. West loses his temper when ordered to open up a second front against a German position beyond Lone Tree, a well-known Loos landmark, where there was uncut wire. Striking him as 'the quintessence of criminal stupidity', he explodes with rage at Maddison's reaction, ordering the 'horrible little gas-merchant' to take the grin off his face.

> The London Division is over there, he stabs the air towards the Double Crassier. They are on the extreme right. They have got into the Hun front line with little opposition, but have had to stop to make a defensive flank, because the French next to them haven't started yet. Don't ask me why! They have not yet started! That is a fact! So the Londoner's advance is stopped; while the Scottish Division next to us are going strong towards Loos. Their left flank is exposed, because we are held up.

The American writer, James Hall, describes vividly the early hours of Tuesday morning shattered by a 'two-hundred-piece orchestra of blacksmiths with sledgehammers beating kettle-drums the size of brewery vats that might have approximated, in quality and volume, the sound of the battle.' The reserves had finally arrived and the fight was on:

> Lurid flashes of light issued from the ground as though a door to the infernal regions had been thrown jarringly open. The cloud of thick smoke was shot through with red gleams. Men ran along the parapet hurling bombs down into the trench.

At once they were hidden by the smoke and then silhouetted in a glare of blinding light. Writing in the cockney vernacular of those around him, the American volunteer heard one Tommy call out 'Fritzie's a tough old bird. 'E's a-go'n' to die game, you got to give it to 'im.' In the urgent calls for more 'lemons' and 'cricket balls', as the hand-held bombs were called, box after box of them, each containing a dozen grenades, were continually passed up the line from hand to hand, but still came the cry for more. Meanwhile, those bombers wounded by their own temperamental devices, and who were able, limped back in twos and threes. One in particular, Hall remembered, was a lad with his eyes covered with a bloody bandage being led back to safety by another with a shattered hand. 'Poor old Tich!' the helper declared, explaining that the grenade went off 'right in 'is face! But you did yer bit, Tich! You ought to 'a' seen 'im, you blokes! Was n't 'e a-lettin'' 'em 'ave it!'

Under the cover of the artillery bombardment when the reserves finally arrived, a huge cheer of 'Hurroo!' went up from the London Irish. As the exhausted attackers turned defenders made their way to the back trenches they were shaken by the hand and relieved of their rifles and kit in gratitude for their astounding effort. The euphoria was only dampened with a roll call of the names of the many read out with no answer. The *Weekly Despatch* witness saw comrades who had 'stood the strain of battle like so many giants crying like children all alone'. While he watched others 'scribble the news of their dramatic escape and how the 1/18th Battalion London Regiment had saved the day', he asked no questions as to why the planned relief failed to arrive on time. The gain of ground appeared insignificant, consisting as it did of one ruined village and a few square miles of fallow land. Although Lens still stood triumphant and untaken, Captain Street reckoned there was much in the Allies' favour. Loos was by no means a victory but it was an exhibition of strength on the part of the Allies. While the losses were deemed to be too great in proportion to the results achieved, it was not certain to him that the outcome would have been much different had more men been flung into the struggle at the critical time. 'Conjecture is unprofitable' he wrote in 1916, hoping that the lesson would be learned that 'men and men alone will terminate this war'. The effects of the 'operations that have been named the Battle of Loos ... will be far more beneficial than those of a spectacular victory', he adds, without the benefit of foresight.

Chapter Seven

A Blighty One

One night after the great charge at Loos, Patrick MacGill happened upon a small squad of Scottish soldiers. On asking if there was any tea going spare he was offered a mug and asked by one of the Scots the name of his outfit, to which he replied the London Irish. ''Twas your fellows that kicked the futba' across the field into the German trench?' asked the Scot. 'Not that far,' answered MacGill, explaining how a bullet hit the ball by the barbed-wire entanglements. 'I saw it lying there during the day' he said. The Scot thought that it was the maddest thing he had ever heard. He then asked if many men were lost, to which MacGill replied 'a good number'.

Later that same evening, back at his own section, the writer famous in his day as 'the Navvy Poet' happened upon a comrade preparing breakfast and accepted the invitation to join him. Again the conversation turned to the numbers who died that day. MacGill's host remembered one who was killed the moment he was over the top. 'He had only one kick of the ball,' he recalled, 'before a bullet caught him in the stomach and brought him down along with many others.' Just a few days later and Patrick MacGill's own name would be recorded in the 'Green Book', that revered record containing amongst thousands of others entries for Frank Edwards, Geoffrey Belton Cobb and whoever was the *Weekly Despatch*'s anonymous commentator. The 'Green Book' contained the names of all those who had received a 'Blighty One', an injury serious enough to mean a passage home.

Medical facilities at Loos included sixteen advanced dressing stations, fifteen main dressing stations and thirteen casualty clearing stations. In all, these units could accommodate just over 11,500 casualties at any on time. Seventeen ambulance trains were also provided, as were canal barges and road transport to evacuate wounded men towards the coast. All in all this represented wholly inadequate arrangements to cope smoothly with the tens of thousands of casualties

43. Patrick MacGill.

there were. As a stretcher-bearer, Patrick McGill was very much aware that the front line infantry battalions were able only to provide the most superficial medical care. Close to the front line in a support or reserve trench, was the regimental aid post, attended by the Battalion Medical Officer, his orderlies and stretcher-bearers. The facilities were crude and limited, often only providing casual respite for casualties before they were moved on to an advanced dressing station. The walking wounded did just that, while others were carried out by hand carriage or on wheeled stretchers. It would be a year after Loos that relay posts for stretcher-bearers were established every 1,000 yards or so along the line, and to avoid congestion, specific trench systems allocated for the removal of casualties.

With a serious wound to his thigh and unable to walk, Frank Edwards was stretchered to the nearest advance dressing station (ADS). Better equipped than the regimental aid post, the ADS was still only able to provide limited medical treatment. Frank's leg, and probably his life, was saved in an emergency operation to halt the bleeding from the severed artery in his thigh. He was one of the lucky ones. Following the carnage that was Loos, the volume of casualties soon overwhelmed the primitive provisions, with thousands of wounded men lying on stretchers in the open for hours. From the ADS, a wagon, or even a London omnibus, would have taken Frank to a casualty clearing station (CCS), the first large scale, well-equipped medical facility where his condition would be assessed. These stations took of the form of either a tented camp or, where conditions allowed, an establishment of huts. All were set a few miles behind the lines close to a railway line. As one of the 1,000 or so casualties coming through at any one time, Frank's condition was assessed as either treatable for return to the Front, ruled unfit for further travel or admission to one of the general hospitals located near the Army's principal bases at Boulogne, Le Havre, Rouen, Le Touquet and Etaples.

In 1915, half the men wounded sustained a coveted 'Blighty One', but as the war moved on, more were returned to their unit, with the numbers of those deemed fit for duty tending to fluctuate with the demands of the battlefield. After Loos, death on the grand scale would become something of a foregone conclusion. James Hall paints a unique picture of life at the Front in his book *Kitchener's Mob*. In his often comical, but compassionately written accounts, the cockney twang of his fellow 9th Battalion Royal Fusiliers is spelled out phonetically to add a genuine sense of atmosphere. Like the dialogue taken from an old documentary film, his prose captures the tone and general banter to put into context the cavalier attitude among fellow Tommies about the dubious blessings of getting wounded. 'I'm a-go'n' to arsk fer a nice Blightey one!' declares one of Hall's contemporaries. 'Four months in Brentford 'ospital an' me Christmas puddin' as Well!'

'Now, don't ferget, you blokes!' exclaims another, 'County o' London War 'Ospital fer me if I gets a knock! Write it on a piece o' pyper an' pin it to me tunic w'en you sends me back to the ambulance.' A wounded Tommy then hobbles past on one foot, supporting himself against the side of the trench. 'Got a Blightey one' he boasts gleefully. 'Solong, you lads! I'll be with you again arter the 'olidays.'

Best known as co-author of the *Bounty Trilogy*, which later spawned the *Mutiny on the Bounty* films, James Hall further explains:

> Those who do not know the horrors of modern warfare cannot readily understand the joy of the soldier at receiving a wound which is not likely to prove serious. A bullet in the arm or the shoulder, even though it shatters the bone, or a piece of shrapnel or shell casing in the leg, was always a matter for congratulation. These were Blightey [sic] wounds. When Tommy received one of this kind, he was a candidate for hospital in Blightey, as England is affectionately called. For several months he would be far away from the awful turmoil. His body would be clean; he would be rid of the vermin and sleep comfortably in a bed at night. The strain would be relaxed, and, who knows, the war might be over before he was again fit for active service. And so the less seriously wounded made their way painfully but

cheerfully along the trench, on their way to the field dressing-station, the motor ambulance, the hospital ship, and – home, while their un-wounded comrades gave them words of encouragement and good cheer.

'Good luck to you, Sammy boy!' one comrade calls to a wounded pal. 'If you sees my missus, tell 'er I'm as right as rain!' Another proclaims Sammy to be a 'lucky blighter!' and calls for him to "'ave a pint of ale at the W'ite Lion fer me' while he is convalescing. 'An' a good feed o' fish an' chips fer me, Sammy' demands another before spotting a second familiar face. "Ere comes old Sid! Where you caught it, mate?' he asks. 'In me bloomin' shoulder,' Sid replies. 'It ain't 'arf givin' it to me!' But his discomfort is received with little sympathy. 'Never you mind, Sid! Blightey fer you, boy!' As he makes his way painfully through the admitting ranks, the list of demands continues. 'Hi, Sid!' calls out another face from the streets of Poplar. 'Tell me old lady I'm still up an' comin', will you? You know w'ere she lives, forty-six Bromley Road.'

Perhaps having endured a similar barrage of good-natured repartee from his pals, Frank Edwards eventually found himself on board a Red Cross truck on 27 September 1915, bound for General Headquarters, Etaples. Two days later, after delousing, a bath and for the first time in six months a soft bed to sleep in, pyjamas and clean sheets, he was woken early one morning by a nurse shining a torch in his face telling him he was to go home. He was then brought a parcel of clothes and a few hours later he found himself at Calais Harbour boarding a hospital ship bound for Southampton. His name was entered into a book and he was issued with a postcard to inform his pals that he was well and the name of his assigned hospital.

Throughout Britain many hospitals were civilian facilities or requisitioned buildings turned over to military use. But such was the sheer numbers of casualties flowing in from the various theatres of war that the nation's carefully planned medical facilities were soon overwhelmed. At the outbreak of war the British Red Cross Society and the Order of St John of Jerusalem combined to form the Joint War Committee under the protection of the Red Cross emblem. With buildings secured, equipment found and staff deployed, many temporary hospitals were made available throughout Britain to treat servicemen wounded abroad. Town halls, schools and large private houses were also brought into use where they could be found. The larger establishments became auxiliary hospitals attached to central military hospitals, which directed the movement of the patients who remained under military control.

In all, there were over 3,000 auxiliary hospitals administered under county directors and usually staffed by a commandant who was in charge of the hospital structure but not the medical and nursing services. A quartermaster was responsible for provisions and a matron was in charge of the nursing staff, including members of the local Voluntary Aid Detachment who were trained

44. A casualty clearing station.

45. Entrained to a general hospital.

46. Taken aboard a hospital ship.

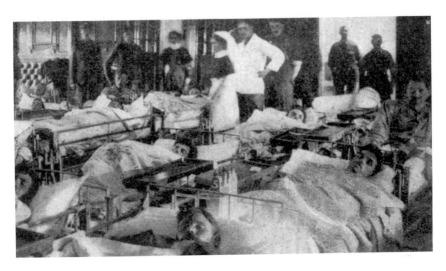

47. The journey home.

in first aid and home nursing. These were usually local part-time women volunteers, although paid labour was available for cooks and other ancillary staff. Medical attendance was provided locally and on a voluntary basis. The patients at these hospitals were generally the less seriously wounded or those in need of convalescence like Frank. Servicemen generally preferred these auxiliary hospitals where the discipline was not as strict as their military counterparts and conditions were less crowded and the surroundings more homely.

★ ★ ★

Frank Edwards spent almost a year convalescing, from 29 September 1915 to 24 August 1916. Although the gunshot wound to his thigh eventually healed, the effects of gas poisoning would affect him for the rest of his life. His general recovery, however, was remarkably good and eventually his sporting prowess was used to good effect. Over the course of the following two years he qualified as a gymnastics instructor, lifesaver and physical culture expert. One newspaper report has him employed at St Dunstan's, the famous hostel for blinded service personnel founded in February 1915. Sixteen soldiers were initially installed in an elegant eighteenth-century mansion pleasantly situated in six-and-a-half acres by Regent's Park in London. Much of the grounds were made over to workshops and classrooms for teaching Braille, typewriting, knitting, basket making, mat making, boot repair, carpentry, poultry farming, telephone operating and massage.

Physiotherapy played an important role at this time in the recovery of many wounded servicemen, and selected homes such as those run by St Dunstan's organised physical training and remedial exercise classes under the supervision of Army physical training instructors. Sporting activities included running and walking races, cricket ball throwing, putting the shot, the long jump, rowing and cycling, all aided either by wires or the assistance of a sighted person. Football was played at a basic level, kicking penalties against a sighted goalkeeper. A system of putting a bell inside the ball as a team game did not succeed.

Frank's actual role in all of this is not clear. According to St Dunstan's archivist, the role of Sports Organiser accredited him by the newspaper did not exist before 1919. As a medal-winning gymnast in his youth and an able swimmer, Frank may have been seconded to one of St Dunstan's growing number of centres on transfer back to his regiment. His service record shows him appointed lance corporal in December 1916 and on 27 January 1917 promoted to the rank of corporal. In June of that year, while at Winchester with the 18th Reserve Battalion London Irish Rifles, he was made acting sergeant with pay, and by the end of August had been awarded the first of two Physical Training and Instructors Certificates, the other on 6 February 1918. He was variously stationed at Hadham, Crystal Palace and Hitchin before discharge on 5 February 1919.

48. Retraining at St Dunstan's Hostel for Blinded Soldiers and Sailors.

49. Old Comrades Dinner of the London Irish Rifles, 1923.

Although the Armistice was declared on 11 November 1918, peace treaty negotiations continued until July 1919, which marked the official end to the war and when Frank returned to his parents' home in Chelsea to continue with his life in Civvie Street. His wife and child were by now dead six years and Frank clearly found life in the military more appealing than that of a stationer's clerk. On 6 August 1919 he re-enlisted in the Military Foot Police a month shy of 26 years old, holding the rank of Acting Lance Corporal and was posted to 'Lousy Hounslow', the disparaging description of Hounslow Cavalry Barracks in West Middlesex.

Dating from 1791, it originally followed on in the tradition begun in the seventeenth century of Army and Navy hospitals. Come the catastrophic results of early twentieth-century warfare and some of the men passing through here still carried with them the lice and other parasites acquired at the Front. Although not a hospital in the modern sense of the word, the facility was inspired by Louis XIV's Hotel des Invalides in Paris and the Royal Hospital at Kilmainham, Dublin, both designed to accommodate retired and disabled servicemen in magnificent surroundings at a time when arrangements for the sick and wounded were still at their most primitive. In addition to medical and surgical wards, these hospitals included small wards for officers, prisoners, lunatics, ophthalmic cases and those suffering from venereal disease and scabies. The separate block plan was inappropriate for small regimental hospitals, which ideally comprised an administrative core with attached ward wings, arranged in line. One of the best-preserved examples of the type, a sixty-bed hospital set into the 1861 barrack complex remains the oldest still in use by the British Army. The facilities provided today include a gym and various sports and recreational activities that would have ideally suited Frank's remedial experience and his new calling of gym instructor.

On 23 June 1921, Frank extended his service to 12 years. Four months later he married Susannah Ansell, a local widow four years his senior with a 12-year-old daughter, Queenie. On the wedding certificate, Frank declares for the first time his true marital status as that of widower. Georgina, his first wife, would have been 26 years old and their child eight, had they survived. It was Christmas 1911 when Georgina's sister, Lily, gave her an autograph book. In it are various dedications and verses from family and colleagues at the Census Office in London where Georgina worked until May 1912. Included in its pages is a naive watercolour of a vase of flowers painted after 1918 and signed 'F. Edwards, Footballer of Loos'. Clearly, this relic was precious to Frank, as the only tangible memento of young lives lost when he was himself little more than a boy.

Frank and Susannah had a daughter, Lily Ruby, who was born at Hounslow Barracks on 25 March 1922. The family then transferred to Aldershot Command where Frank was appointed lance corporal on 1 April. He passed his Senior Certificate of Instruction in Military Police duties at Mytchett and Hythe where he gained his certificate to use a revolver. By February 1923, he and his young family had transferred to Shornecliffe Camp, the army barracks at Sandgate, near Folkestone on the south coast of Kent. In May that same year an Old Comrades Dinner of the London Irish Rifles was held at the Manchester Hotel in London. Featured in a press photograph of the occasion is Lieutenant Colonel E. C. Concanon, DSO who commanded the regiment at Loos. A chef hands him on a plate the 'historic football' used at the battle when they went over the top. 'Much significance attached this football' the short press release adds, 'when the Rifles went over the top, they kicked this sphere ahead of them; kicked it so that the Germans could realise what they thought of bullets.' Unfortunately the headline credits the 'Irish Rifles Guards' and the brief text makes no mention of Edwards.

Frank and his family remained at Shornecliffe for the next three years until moving back to Aldershot where Frank was promoted to the rank of sergeant and where he qualified as a fencing instructor. He had a son, also called Frank, who was born on 1 February 1926. Twenty-six days later and the proud father took part in the ceremony marking the amalgamation of the Military Foot Police and the Military Mounted Police to form the Corps of Military Police. His Royal Highness the Prince of Wales was Colonel-in-Chief of the Middlesex Regiment at the time when Aldershot was a hot bed of sporting competitions of every description. Famously abdicating as King Edward VIII a decade later and subsequently made Duke of Windsor, Aldershot clearly held some happy memories for the him. A letter sent by the Duke's private secretary to Frank in 1952 expresses how much his Royal Highness appreciated the 'interesting photograph which recalled happy memories'. This photograph (sadly lost) was taken in 1926, the year after the organisers of the spectacular Wembley Searchlight Tattoo failed entirely to mark the 10th anniversary of the Battle of Loos.

50. Hounslow Cavalry Barracks.

Chapter Eight

Man of Loos

Torchlight Revues were the military fetes that took the name as part of a tradition dating back to 1894 when General HRH the Duke of Connaught (later Field Marshall and Honorary Colonel of the London Irish Rifles, and Queen Victoria's third son) arranged at GOC Aldershot, a military display for the Queen's entertainment. When darkness fell the military bands amassed to perform by lit torches held aloft by ranks of soldiers. As the event became more elaborate each year, so a programme developed to include twenty-three musical items comprising 1,500 bandsmen, pipers and buglers, sporting events and displays of the latest military innovations spread over four successive evenings. With the increasing use of electricity, the fete changed its name in 1921 to The Searchlight Tattoo and included displays of illuminated aerial combat and a selected theme. Otherwise, the programme remained largely a musical affair, including the proverbial Musical Ride.

As part of the Wembley Exhibition in 1925 the tattoo held there included the first true historic pageants that were the forerunners to the more elaborate, but now defunct, Royal Tournament. Trenches were dug and dramatic effects laid on as a tribute to those who had fought in France. Great unwieldy tanks rolled across the uneven ground spewing flames and smoke into lines of a terrified foe that had never before seen the like. Blinding flashes of light and ear-splitting blasts from thunder flashes shook the vast arena from pillar to post and the shriek of whistles pierced the deafening roar as officers led the way over the top through a hail of lead towards the enemy lines. Breaching the vicious barbed wire amid the smoke, explosions and the rattle of machine-gun fire, ranks of young men roared their way into the German trenches where they dispatched what was left of the Hun with cold steel. So popular was this extravaganza that it was extended a full month from 24 August to 31 October, marking proudly and magnificently the major offensives on the Western Front, except the first, at Loos, the first Great Push.

As far as can be established there was no anxiety expressed on the part of the London Irish Rifles or any unit of the 47th Division regarding this exclusion. Perhaps the sight of strange, goggle-eyed hoods covering the heads of British troops was deemed less savoury than fresh-faced warriors looking directly into the whites of Fritz's eyes. Filling the vast arena with thick yellow smog to simulate the clouds of poisonous gas might have lowered the ideal of an otherwise wholesome and noble entertainment. Asphyxiating gas was still something of an indelible stain on an already deeply soiled conflict.

The sense of unease at the use of this diabolical new weapon was refuelled with the post-war revelation that much decision-making was delegated to Major Charles Foulkes who was a relatively minor figure in the hierarchy. The use of chlorine and later other toxic chemicals as weapons had resulted in a public outcry at home and across the Atlantic. General Peyton March of the US Army condemned the use of gas as an indiscriminate weapon that eroded the principle of non-combatant immunity. Sir John French deplored gas as an 'impolite weapon', rendering all the combative skills of the good soldier useless. After war the League of Nations was left to restore the international control of warfare. The use of chemical weapons had made a nonsense of the Hague Convention, and public reaction was likewise vehement in its condemnation of their use. Also, the lack of munitions forcing the British to use asphyxiating gas for the first time may have sat uncomfortably as part of the heroic public display.

If not resentment, then certainly a measure of disappointment must have greeted the indifference afforded the London Irish Regimental Association as it commemorated the tenth anniversary of Loos in 1925. In his book *The Great Push*, Patrick MacGill recalls their remarkable advance. 'The instinct of self-preservation is the strongest in created beings' he wrote, having seen hundreds of men concentrated on their own personal safety. 'Moving forward to attack with the nonchalance of a church parade', he wondered if the men who kicked the football were the most nervous. But he did not believe 'for a second that the ball was brought for that purpose'. More likely, he reasoned, that they had it to take their minds off the horror ahead of them and the 'dread anticipation of death'. The idea was to take the game to the enemy, to shock them with something outrageous.

It should have been the stuff of history, but it was not to be. It was an audacious action in an ignominious affair. That some form of recognition was due came down to members of the London Irish Rifles Regimental Association, who decided to mark the occasion themselves, albeit a year later, on 24 September 1926, in the spacious grounds of their Duke of York's Headquarters in Chelsea where the charge of the London Irish at Loos would be re-enacted as the climax to the 'pageantry and thrilling war games' comprising the regiment's own Torchlight Tattoo. On the three nights the pageant was performed, the *West London News* reported attendances of over 8,000 spectators, with crowds thronging the pavements outside trying to catch a glimpse of the spectacle.

Following the sounding of the First Post, bands entered the ground lit up by the powerful glare of four searchlights. Irish National Dances accompanied by pipers continued on from a smart drill display. The pageant play that followed told the history of the London Irish Rifles across four periods, ending with the Tommies of The Great War and the dimming down of the searchlights for the entry of a detachment carrying brightly burning torches. As well as performing what were described as 'intricate evolutions in the centre of the ground', the Transport Section gave a burlesque version of the Musical Ride as well as a military musical fantasia to bugle and drum. After an amusing and well-received impression of barrack life from Reveille to Lights Out, it was time to re-enact 'The Attack at Loos' as the thrilling finale. Invited to don the uniform of his old regiment and to re-enact the bold episode was the 'mad footballer' himself, Frank Edwards.

The scene was set on the great bare plain, with small villages at rare intervals breaking the monotony of the flat landscape. Gaunt pylons intensified the melancholy of a countryside dominated by great slag heaps, a more unpromising scene for a great offensive battle hardly imaginable. The crowd sat hushed as first light on 25 September 1915 came alive again to the boom of guns, the whistling of shells and the crack of rifle shots, all realistically reproduced to send shudders down the spines of the spectators. A heavy cloud straddled the ragged line of trenches. If this dismayed public sensibilities then it went unreported. The men of the 1st Battalion London Irish Rifles were ready, awaiting the order to charge. Rifleman Edwards fumbled in his haversack before cautiously drawing out what appeared to be a crumpled leather bag. 'Blimey, you've still got it!' muttered the man next to him. Orders were about to be disobeyed but there was nothing to lose. The honour of leading the attack had fallen to the men of the London Irish. Putting the ball to his lips, Edwards began to blow. At 6.30am the cry echoed along the line: 'Over you go, lads and the best of luck!' With his rifle in one hand, Frank sent the football towards the German lines. To the cry of 'On the ball, London Irish', the audience watched spellbound as the leather ball was dribbled forward from man to man until 'finally a goal was scored!'

This dramatic reconstruction of the battle may have provided the inspiration for London based film director, Sinclair Hill, who penned the first draft of the most ambitious war film to date in the same year designed to save the ailing Stoll Picture Production Company. Hill learned his trade at Italy's Turin Studios, where the output was far more artistically and technically advanced than the vast majority of material manufactured by the British studios. As the

51. The London Irish Rifles Regimental Association Tattoo, 1926.

company's one constant and most prolific operator, Hill was made managing director, which allowed him the opportunity to modernise their film style and showcase his real capabilities. One of the last features of the silent era, the film would be entitled *The Guns of Loos* and star Henry Victor as John Grimlaw, a ruthless armaments manufacturer in love with Diana, played by Madeline Carroll in her film debut, who is in turn drawn to Clive (Donald McArdle). Her affections waver between both men as they march off to the battlefields of France. At the front and under fire, Grimlaw loses his nerve, but is brought back from the brink by his rival, going on to courageously save his battery, losing his eyesight in the process. Back home, Grimlaw bravely stands up to strikers at his old factory, which greatly impresses Diana, who chooses him as her husband.

In her book, *Reframing British Cinema, 1918–1928: Between Restraint and Passion*, Christine Gledhill rebuffs the criticism that these early screen productions are too stagey. She celebrates the staginess as a fascinating aspect of British cinema in so far as theatricality transcends class. This is true in an episode before the battle where as part of the show one of them men performs in drag, perhaps inspired by Frank Edwards and his pals who danced through the streets of Maroc wearing liberated women's dresses and frock coats before the battle. Otherwise the business of class looms large in the film as a pastiche of life on the factory floor and on the battlefield where the autocratic Grimlaw is proved to be a thoroughly good egg.

The Guns of Loos is also highly political in that it follows the fortunes of an armaments manufacturer who subsequently leads an artillery battery starved of shells as a result of the demands of a government ill-prepared for such an onslaught. As the war progressed so, it became increasingly clear that private companies could not cope with the demand, partly because they were too small or could not source enough metal and other raw materials. To ensure an uninterrupted flow of shells, the British government enacted the 1915 Munitions of War Act, under which it became a penal offence for a worker to leave their current job to work for another firm without the consent of his employer or to refuse to undertake a new job, regardless of the rates of pay on offer. Workers were not allowed to refuse to work overtime, whether paid or not. With trade union leadership proving weak in protecting workers from belligerent employers, this in turn led to the more politically motivated resisting what they saw as draconian wartime state policies. This state of affairs acts as a sub-plot to *The Guns of Loos* where at one point Grimlaw's battery is left with just a single shell with which to respond to the German guns.

Produced at Cricklewood Studios, then the largest facility in Britain, the Loos battlefield was partly recreated in Gibbs Pit, West Thurrock, Kent, which is today the site of Lakeside Shopping Centre. This earliest full-length war movie was shot on an epic scale, with hundreds of extras and troupes of mounted-gunners at the gallop creating some memorable early screen action moments. The early part of the tale centres on Grimlaw in the role of a forward observation officer. In a confused mix of fact and fiction, the battle begins after a caption bearing the ominous date 25 September 1915 fades from the screen. While little is made of the great pre-assault artillery bombardment, the gas cloud creeping over battlefield is laboured, as though to underline its unwelcome intrusion onto the field of battle. The only lines of infantry shown waiting for the signal to charge are the Scots, who become disorientated by the gas cloud carried back by the wind. They are eventually rallied by Piper Daniel Laidlaw, playing himself in the film as the Piper of Loos, standing high above the parapet rousing his comrades, oblivious to his own safety, advancing wounded until the first objective is captured.

The opening caption to the film promisingly declares that the name of the small mining village of Loos in northern France would secure its place in history because of the great battle fought there. Yet the days and weeks of fighting are confined to a matter of hours wherein the battle is quickly won and the village of Loos easily captured. The Germans rally with the British guns unable to respond, not because of a lack of reserves, but due to a shortage of shells. This links to the front page story of a national newspaper dated 27 December 1915, which was devoted to the Minister of Munitions, David Lloyd George, dealing with the civic unrest amongst munitions workers. More like a propaganda film made during the conflict, the core messages of duty and respect serve to baffle any historical significance. The film opened in Brighton in 1928 to excellent notices, although the effort failed to save Stoll Pictures. Frank Edwards was posted in Wiesbaden at the time.

★ ★ ★

In 1931, the Belfast correspondent of the *Irish Times* reported on the arrival of the London Irish Rifles to undertake its annual training period in Northern Ireland, the first English territorial battalion (as it was now described) to do so. With the Northern Ireland government about to move into new buildings at Stormont and the Irish Republican Army declared an illegal organisation in the Irish Free State, the links made by that newspaper between the London Irish and the Royal Ulster Rifles were at this point in time somewhat premature. It would not be until 1937 that the London Regiment was disbanded to create The London Irish Rifles (The Royal Ulster Rifles). The London Irish would be raised into two battalions in 1939 and after the Second World War, embodied as 1st Battalion London Irish Rifles (Royal Ulster Rifles).

In 1967 the reorganization of the Territorial Army would reduce the London Irish to company strength, the three regular Irish line infantry regiments combining to form the Royal Irish Rangers, with D Company (London Irish Rifles) the 4th Battalion until the re-formation of the London Regiment in 1993. Quite where the *Irish Times* came by the seeds of such advancements is not clear, although a cynic might conclude that the London Territorials found themselves in 1931 unwittingly embroiled in gesture politics. At the official reception, the then Commander of the London Irish Rifles, Lieutenant Colonel J. Allan Mulholland, thanked the people of Belfast for the tremendous welcome they had extended the Londoners, which he boldly considered to be equal to that of a Royal visit.

There then followed a presentation by Lieutenant Colonel Mulholland to the Mayor of Belfast, Sir Crawford McCullagh, of a small replica of what the *Irish Times* described as 'the famous statue' of the Footballer of Loos. The mayor said that it would remind the people of Belfast of when the London Irish 'came to stay'. Readers were informed that this was the fourth occasion upon which such a replica was struck, 'marking the proud part filled by the regiment in one of the finest actions of the Great War'. The original, together with the battered leather football, occupied a place of honour in the regimental mess. The original statuette, Mulholland explained, was designed and cast by a member of the regiment and epitomised the moment the London Irish went over the top 'when the regiment had really first leapt into universal fame'. The name of Frank Edwards had no part in this. The focus was clearly on the deed and not the individual. This becomes demonstrably clear from the London Irish Regimental Memorial recording the names of fallen comrades in the two world wars. To the right of the central dedication tablet is positioned a bronze statuette of a Second World War soldier dubbed 'Son of the Man'. To the left of the tablet is the original statuette of the First World War Tommy charging forward holding a rifle in one hand and a football in the other. It no longer holds the 'universal fame' as *The Footballer*, but as '*Man* of Loos'. This alteration was made sometime after 1966, probably to link the same valiant spirit passed down from the 'Man' to the 'Son'.

The major factor in Frank Edwards' relegation to non-league history, however, was the late arrival of the 1st Battalion regimental history – in 1931 it was still very much a work in progress. In his book, *Signal Corporal*, Ernest May states that he first suggested writing the story of the 2nd Battalion London Irish Rifles in the First World War at a meeting of the Regimental Association in 1926, the year of the Chelsea Tattoo. The proposal was received with enthusiasm and the former captain was charged with collecting the information ready for 'someone skilled in writing' to turn out the book. Forty years later and on his retirement in 1968, May began the work himself and *Signal Corporal* was published four years later. In his unpublished account of the 1st Battalion, former Second Lieutenant S. F. Major maintains that it was decided in 1933 by the Old Comrades Association to write a 1914–18 history of the 1st and 2nd Battalions London Irish Rifles. Major was duly appointed Secretary, 1st Battalion History, and although work began a year later, it would not see completion for another 38 years. In the Foreword, Major's son suggests that Ernest May was either not as lucky or so assiduous as his father. He claims that the general consensus of those originally approached sixteen years after the battle was that it was 'rather late in the day for there to be a history'. Perhaps this was the reason for Major's delay. May, however, persevered, receiving on publication 57 years later an enthusiastic response from Major General Sir Ralph Hone, the colourful Crown and Colonial Counsel who joined the London Irish Rifles in 1915. Hone had always considered the Official War Diaries 'too brief and

52. The Footballer
of Loos statuette.

uncommunicative'. Indeed, the war diarist himself agreed, feeling that the result gave him no real satisfaction and was convinced that the net result was 'utterly inadequate'.

In his Foreword to May's book, published in 1972, Sir Ralph states he found it a matter of regret that there had been no published history of the separate achievements of both battalions in the First World War, but that Ernest May had managed a 'lively and very human war record'. Clearly a labour of love over half a century, the book was viewed as a valuable and interesting contribution to the regiment's gallant and glorious history. Former Second Lieutenant S. F. Major meanwhile had obtained first-hand accounts and recollections of comrades 'as were available at the time', seeing his work as more of a supplement to the History of the 47th (London) Division published in

1922. It was a highly demanding task involving 'much cross checking amongst comrades for correctness and approval', with work ceasing in October 1939 in the belief there was insufficient material to merit publication. Like May, however, Major took up the challenge again on retirement many years later, eventually completing the work in 1971 when his *War History of the 1/18th Battalion London Regiment* was presented to the Imperial War Museum. Curiously a copy was not presented to the London Irish Rifles Regimental Museum, nor was its existence known to them until research was underway for the writing of this account.

Certainly by 1935, Major had fully documented the 1st Battalion's finest hour at Loos. For in that year, commemorating the 20th anniversary of the battle, the London *Evening News* was running a series of feature articles on the history of the London Irish Rifles, culminating in the fabled footballing adventure. Credited as a history in progress, former Second Lieutenant Major laid out the first, fully documented account of the regiment's actions, complete with eyewitness reports confirming Frank Edwards as the contriver and executioner of the audacious soccer action.

The BBC then invited Edwards to Broadcasting House in London to tell listeners how he and his comrades fought their way through the clouds of poisonous gas and waves of machine-gun fire to play out the plan. Listening to the 'thrilling narrative of the historic act' was Edwards' former pal and the man who saved his life, ex-rifleman Micky Mileham. A few weeks later and the two men were reunited after twenty years. Although Mileham had been a teetotaller all that time, one newspaper reported the two men drinking 'a hearty toast to each other in a glass of beer as they relived those tense moments and the renewal of their war-time friendship'.

Also listening from his home in Nottingham had been Captain Dale who was given Edwards' address through the BBC. This was the young officer who had put a bullet through other footballs before the charge. Frank, as one of the thousands of servicemen to receive a football donated by readers of a national newspaper, explained that his love of the game ensured he carried a ball with him everywhere. This combined with the grim awareness of what lay ahead provided a golden opportunity to give the Hun his biggest shock since the war began. The *Newbury Herald* and the *Reading Mercury* reported the 'thrilling narrative' of the Maidenhead man (where Edwards was living) who kicked a football during a bayonet charge. 'Just imagine, as I did' Edwards recounted to the listeners, 'a party of London Irishmen, with our war cry of "Hurroo" charging across No Man's Land passing the ball forward to finish up the mad rush by leaping into their trench with the rifle and bayonet'.

1959 was the centenary year of the London Irish Regiment. In his capacity as the chairman of the Centenary Committee, Major-General

53. *The London Evening News*, 25 September 1935.

Sir Ralph Hone wondered how the anniversary should be commemorated. The plan, started in 1957, was for Special Parades on Loos Sunday (27 September) and Remembrance Sunday (8 November), an Officers' Ball at the Mansion House, a Sergeant's Ball at Caxton Hall, a Regimental Association Dinner and a second Officers' Dinner at the Duke of York's Headquarters, and an All Ranks' Regimental Ball at Chelsea Town Hall, which Frank Edwards attended. A 'Brochure' was published to extol the past exploits of the Regiment and to pay tribute to those across a century who had helped create its high reputation in peace and war. In the history of the Regiment, written by Lieutenant-Colonel Corbally, such a tribute was paid to 1st/18th Londons who, in the vanguard of the attack of their brigade made history by dribbling a football before them across No Man's Land. 'This gallant and light-hearted gesture, instigated by the Battalion football team' was said to have greatly appealed to the popular imagination, with the football now treasured in the Regimental Museum. An exhibit label once accompanying the football was recently unearthed, possibly dating from this time. It names Frank Edwards as the rifleman who first kicked the ball towards German lines, but it was again down to the London *Evening News* in a special two-part feature about 'the Saturday afternoon soldiers' to appeal to popular imagination and maintain the record of events.

54. *The London Evening News, 17 November 1959.*

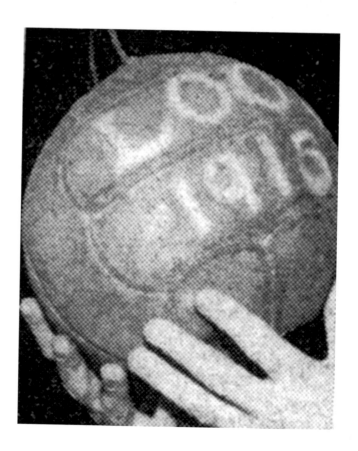

55. The Loos football, 1964.

THE LOOS FOOTBALL, 1915

On 25 Sept 1915, in the trenches opposite Loos, Rfn
F Edwards of the London Irish Rifles took a football from
his pack and inflated it. When ordered over the top, he put
on his gas mask, and, rifle in hand, kicked the ball towards
the German lines. His comrades joined in and although
Rfn Edwards fell wounded, others kicked the ball on until
first one trench, then another and finally Loos itself was
taken

56. London Irish Rifles Regimental Museum exhibition tag *c.*1960.

Come 1964 and Frank's death lid sparked controversy amongst some veterans of Loos who expressed doubts as to whether he was indeed the rifleman who first kicked the football into battle. 'It's a pile of piffle and nonsense that Edwards rallied the men through his football' claimed Bert Coward, himself a veteran rifleman. He told the *News of the World* in no uncertain terms that as the assistant curator of the London Irish Museum and Secretary of the London Irish Rifles he knew for sure that there was 'not a living man who could say they know the actual man who kicked off the ball'. A colleague pointing to the battered football bearing the inscription etched in chalk 'Loos 1915', believed it to be the actual ball kicked into No Man's Land. He confirmed that nobody was given the credit for kicking off the football 'because we're not sure'. But then former rifleman Walter Dalby was sure. From his home in Harlington, Middlesex, he spoke up in Edwards' defence, declaring he was in no doubt that Frank was the first solider to kick the ball. 'There's no question about it' he exclaimed,

> because I was the second man to kick it. I was 17 at the time. We all had footballs, but a Lieutenant [sic] Dale put a bullet through mine, saying it would distract us. He didn't get Frankie's however. Frankie pulled out the football just as we were going over the top. He took the first kick, and sent it to me.

But those in charge of what they believed to be the official version of events were not to be swayed. The football eventually made its way permanently to the Officers' Mess and the accompanying tag to a drawer where it remains to this day.

★ ★ ★

57. *The News of the World*, February 1964.

In 1966, the *London Evening Standard* ran a feature on 'London's doomed battalions' prompted by an alleged government threat to axe the Territorials. 'In Place of Honour – A Football' headlined the piece above a picture of Lieutenant Colonel Hood, Commanding Officer of the London Irish Rifles, pictured holding the bronze statuette of the 1915 soldier then still known as 'The Footballer of Loos'. Readers were informed that there was a football on the mantelpiece of the regiment based at The Duke of York's Headquarters. Faded chalk, barely discernable, spelt out *Loos 1915*. 'Suddenly one realises that here is a tangible witness of the truth of legend' suggested the report, for this was the very football that an 'unknown soldier of the London Irish Rifles threw down and dribbled to head an attack on the German trenches at the battle of Loos'. The battered leather relic was witness enough, with the testimony of those witnesses clearly out of step with the regimental archivists.

Had the regimental history of the 1st Battalion been written half a century earlier then things might be different. Philip Warner's account of the Battle of Loos would have been all the more comprehensive if only to determine that the 1/18th did not charge kicking a rugby ball and the East Surreys was not the first regiment to kick a football over the top. Niall Cherry might have added more than photographs of the battered football and the bleak panorama over which it was dribbled and passed. Michael Foreman's *War Game* has been criticised for being too sanitised with regard to the savagery of the First World War. Perhaps, but then it is essentially a work for children and no less moving and compelling for that, typifying the lost lives of millions of young men. His stunning illustrations capture the bleak detail and machinery of that war, but at the expense of fiction over fact in a fusion of the Christmas Truce, the Footballer of Loos and the East Surreys on the Somme.

As has already been explored, the intense interest in the Christmas Truce was driven wholly by letters to the press from troops and loved ones across a long period of time. The reporting of Captain Nevill's exploit on the Somme eased a little of the pain accompanying that murderous debacle. But at Loos, the propaganda machine managed to shroud the ill-fated use of gas by the British for the first time and the failure of British High Command to follow up the success of the attacking divisions. But then with regard to the London Irish there was another factor fermenting uncomfortably in the wings of British history.

Chapter Nine

The Irish Question

In his adventures as an American citizen serving in the British Army during the early months of the First World War, the writer James Norman Hall recalls a part of the front held during the summer of 1915 where the opposing lines of trenches were less than a hundred yards apart. In the early morning when the heavy night mists concealed the lines, some of the men would stand head and shoulders above the parapet and call out: 'Hi, Fritzie!' to which the greeting was returned, 'Hi, Tommy!' and a conversation would ensue. 'Who are you?' the Germans would ask, wanting to know the name of the regiment rather than the individual. A garbled reply of sorts would be followed by a return of the same question. 'We're a battalion of Irish rifles' the Germans liked to answer provocatively, to imply the Irish regiments were disloyal to England and not to be trusted. As a result the British press seized upon every opportunity to applaud Irish regiments and their part in the glorious doings of Empire. That is, except for the London Irish. A month after the Battle of Loos, the *Daily Sketch* devoted its entire back page to 'Irish Eyes Smiling' in a celebration of King and Country (in this case Ireland) facing a common enemy. The leaders both sides of the divide were pictured reaching out the hand of friendship above pictures of the Emerald Isle's finest eagerly marching off to war.

In an unusually candid leader, the editor of *The War Illustrated*, J.A. Hammerton, called upon the leader of the Irish Home Rule Party, John Redmond MP, to write a piece acknowledging the British government's desire to conduct an 'anonymous war', that is one devoid of detail. Hammerton understood that the information process was designed to delude the enemy's ability to identify which British units were fighting and where, but at the time felt that it denied the achievements of individual regiments. 'We have certainly not heard enough about the achievements of the gallant Irish' he declared, describing them as 'notoriously among the best fighters in our Army'. Moreover, and contrary to all expectations, Ireland had so completely answered 'the call of Empire' that it had even taken the Germans by surprise. Within this context, Hammerton appealed to Redmond to share his thoughts, which he did, on 8 January 1916, three months before the Easter Rising in Dublin would in part serve to shatter his premise.

Redmond took as his theme 'The Miracle of Ireland' – a phrase that had been used recently by a leading Unionist journal in England – to describe the amazing transformation which had taken place in the public perception of Ireland since the outbreak of war, a perception based on a turbulent history but one that Redmond believed had now ceased to exist. While acknowledging what he termed 'a difficult relationship', the openly hostile abomination of England was overturned by 'the blessed change' that the war had brought about. The threat to the Empire united Ireland as never before, he claimed, and men of all political views and of all creeds and classes were now in full support, as Ireland saw for herself 'a free and honoured portion of that Empire', as determined as Canada, Australia, New Zealand and South Africa to make the greatest sacrifices in order to protect their own rights. Redmond did, however, recognise that there were 'certain insignificant exceptions, a few individuals who did not share these sentiments. There had been a small number of prosecutions under the Defence of the Realm Act and a handful of seditious acts had been perpetrated, but the greater number of these had taken place on the British mainland. The difference was, he maintained, that the rare events in Ireland were more widely reported.

Two months after the Battle of Loos, *The Daily Sketch* devoted its front page to 'The King's Tribute to Fighting Irishmen'. After 28 days of incessant fighting against huge odds, the 1st Battalion Irish Guards came out less than a company strong with only four officers remaining. This 'glorious tribute to Irish Loyalty and endurance' was duly and formally recognised in a ceremony attended by King George V. On page six of the same newspaper was printed a photograph of a woman and a soldier outside the London Stock Exchange holding a football with the words written on it in chalk: 'Footballers of Loos'. This 'Symbol of Irish Pluck' as the caption proclaimed, was being used as a fundraiser for the London Irish Rifles. This was as good as it got for the London Irish. Only the *Weekly Despatch* fully celebrated how the new regiment's glorious rush and stand at Loos had saved an entire Army Corps and was one of the 'most stirring stories of British grit and courage in the present war'.

The *Weekly Despatch* published its exclusive eyewitness report three weeks after the official ending of the Battle of Loos on 8 October. By then the action was not so much news as history. The costs in terms of numbers of men killed and wounded was known, but the ultimate price in logistics, strategy and leadership had yet to become apparent. Strict censorship on press reporting meant that individual expression had no place in this war, hence the anonymity of the *Despatch's* source. Following the Christmas Truce nine months earlier the British High Command had wisely utilised incredible leniency over what had essentially been a minor rebellion along a great length of the Front and across all ranks. But there would be no such recurrence, no more dallying with accepted standards of behaviour. Orders were orders, which would thereafter be obeyed to the letter and without deviation. Frank Edwards' plan to kick a football ahead of the charge at Loos flew directly in the face of orders. Whereas this may have had some bearing on the wider press, the *Weekly Despatch* used the incident unashamedly to exploit the worth of 'Old Ireland', to the point of caricature.

The source, reportedly a wounded London Irish rifleman recovering in a London hospital bed, was especially erudite, exceedingly well-informed and omnipresent across each strand of the initial offensive. Judging by his unambiguous deference throughout his report to that superior class of man, he was not himself of the warrior elite, but a scholarly individual fiercely proud of his Irish heritage. On first reading of this inspirational and vibrant account, the name Patrick MacGill immediately comes to mind. The popular self-proclaimed 'Navvy Poet' who wrote moving descriptions of his life before, during and after Loos, was himself wounded and evacuated back to London. It is possible that he was persuaded to pen such a cerebral tribute anonymously, perhaps in respect of the sacrifice made by the many thousands of dead and wounded he had left behind. But in this there is an obvious anomaly. In his book *The Amateur Army*, MacGill tells of his experiences as a volunteer with the London Irish Rifles through to embarkation, claiming that he and his colonel were the only two real Irishmen in the battalion. Readers of the *Weekly Despatch*, however, could be forgiven for believing that all London Irish volunteers dug ditches, dreamed of old Ireland and cursed 'begorra' instead of 'blimey!' Then again, both Patrick MacGill and the anonymous narrator shared the same view that the troublesome 'Irish Question' was an issue born of class rather than any nationalistic or religious fervour, and both showed no violent animosity towards Britain and Empire, in fact quite the reverse.

According to the *Despatch's* anonymous narrator, the French were already calling Loos 'a second Fontenoy,' the battle of 1745 where the British infantry earned its reputation for stubborn determination. 'They say it was our brigade that saved the whole British sector' the recovering rifleman expanded. 'But that can hardly be the right title' he added, 'since we Irish were fighting against England at Fontenoy instead of – thank God – for Britain now!' But he understood what the French meant by the comparison and made it clear that on this occasion 'we were Irish, and proud of it and prouder still that we had been able to keep up our fighting reputation.'

FOOTBALL SYMBOL OF IRISH PLUCK

Mrs. Carpet outside the Stock Exchange yesterday collecting for the funds of the London Irish Rifles. It will be remembered that at Loos the London Irish Rifles charged kicking a football in front of them.

58. *The Daily Sketch,* 15 March 1916.

The implication that every London Irish volunteer was Irish, or had a discernable connection with that country, was by no means the case. Born of a meeting held by the Marquis of Donegal on 5 December 1859 at the Freemason's Tavern, Great Queen Street in London (the same venue where the Football Association would be formed four years later) the volunteer rifle corps was originally open to anyone with Irish connections by birth, marriage or property in Ireland. Public anxiety at that time was growing over the possibility of French aggression, which led Lord Derby's government to authorise the formation of such corps throughout the land. With no attack forthcoming from France, most of these brigades disappeared. The London Irish Rifles continued, with shooting practise on Wimbledon Common, resplendent in grey uniforms and shako helmets, more as a social society. For this was also a period of evolution in Irish history when a number of new movements were emerging, aimed at reviving Irish nationalism, including organisations for language, the arts, politics, culture and sport.

At the forefront, with the formation of the Gaelic Athletic Association (GAA) in 1884, was Maurice David, elected as its first president, and Michael Cusack its first secretary. The *Connradh Na Gaeilge* (Gaelic League) – founded in 1893 by Dr Douglas Hyde and Eoin McNeill – sought to restore the Irish language, which was rapidly disappearing due to restrictive laws governing the education of Catholics and as a result of the Great Famine, which had decimated huge swathes of the Gaelic speaking population. The League was met with immediate success and soon almost every parish across Ireland boasted a branch with access to Irish language books. The Local Government Act of 1898 abolished the Grand Juries in Ireland largely made up of the old ruling class, replacing them instead with new democratically elected county councils, which were more representative. Vast improvements in agriculture were also taking place at this time, coupled with a series of land acts that gave native Irish people the right to buy out their own farms.

At the turn of the last century when 100 London Irish Rifles volunteers earned the brigade its first battle honour during the Boer Wars, the two opposing factions of the Irish Parliamentary Party agreed to unite under the leadership of John Redmond, MP for Waterford. A later Parliamentary Act decreed that any Bill, even if rejected by the Lords, would become law after a two-year delay if it passed the Commons a second time in the same parliament.

By 1905, the Irish Literary Renaissance and the Irish National Theatre Society had come about, and the Abbey Theatre was founded in Dublin for the staging of plays by Irish authors. On the political scene, Arthur Griffith founded Sinn Fein as a result of his disappointment with the slow progress of the old Irish Parliamentary Party. Griffith conceived the idea of elected Irish representatives setting up their own parliament in Dublin, an idea that took hold throughout Ireland. A third Home Rule Bill then came before Parliament in 1912 and was again passed in the Commons, only to be rejected once more by the House of Lords. Due to become law in 1914, the situation was tense by March of that year. With the threat of civil unrest, Sir Arthur Paget, commander-in-chief of troops in Ireland, was instructed to move 800 reinforcements in preparation for a possible rebellion in Ulster. Addressing his senior officers at the Curragh, the largest military barracks in Ireland, Paget informed those with homes in Ulster that they could absent themselves without compromising their careers. Others who were not prepared to carry out their duty would be dismissed. Given their predominantly privileged background, the officer class in the British Army mostly sympathised with the Unionists and as a result, 57 of the 70 officers elected for dismissal. What became known as 'The Curragh Mutiny' created huge alarm in government circles, causing Prime Minister Asquith to publicly deny that orders had existed for the repression of the Ulster Unionists and the arrest of their leaders.

The Ulster Unionists believed that the government had intended to crush them but its plan had failed for lack of military support. Government ministers felt that they could not trust the Army to quell opposition to home rule and Irish nationalists were even more doubtful of Asquith's real commitment to granting the Irish self-government. Meanwhile, both volunteer forces were illegally importing arms, with James Connolly elected leader of the Irish Citizens' Army. On the third attempt, the British Parliament passed the Home Rule Bill for Ireland with a special arrangement promised for Ulster, only for attention to switch to Europe and with the outbreak of war the Bill was suspended. The leader of the Irish Parliamentary Party, John Redmond, encouraged the Irish Volunteers to join the war effort, ostensibly for the defence of small nations such as Belgium. But not everyone bought into this. Typical of many a young man at the time either side of the Irish Sea was Tom Barry, who later became Chief of Staff of the IRA in the late 1930s, who wrote:

> In June 1915, in my seventeenth year, I had decided to see what this Great War was like. I cannot plead I went on the advice of John Redmond or any other politician, that if we fought for the British we would secure Home Rule for Ireland, nor can I say I understood what Home Rule meant. I was not influenced by the lurid appeal to fight to save Belgium or small nations. I knew nothing about nations, large or small. I went to the war for no other reason than that I wanted to see what war was like, to get a gun, to see new countries and to feel a grown man.

The Irish Volunteers under Eoin McNeill refused to join the conflict in Europe, preferring instead to maintain an armed force in Ireland to ensure that the British government kept its promise. As a result, the Irish Volunteers movement split and in September 1914, the 36th (Ulster) Division was formed from the Ulster Volunteer Force which raised thirteen battalions for the three Irish regiments based in Ulster, the Royal Inniskilling Fusiliers, the Royal Irish Fusiliers and the Royal Irish Rifles. Although many a Catholic and a Protestant would perish side by side, the motives of the Republicans is perhaps best enshrined by poet-soldier Tom Kettle who was killed on the Somme:

> Know that we the fools, now with the foolish dead,
> Died not for flag, nor King, nor Emperor,
> But for a dream, born in a herdsman's shed,
> And for the secret scripture of the Poor.

At the same time that the Battle of Loos was being fought in France, the Irish Republican Brotherhood (IRB) was being revived to counter the Ulster

Volunteer Force (UVF) founded by Eoin McNeill to prevent Home Rule in Ireland by force if need be. Units of Irish Volunteers were springing up all over the country with companies created and trained according to parish boundaries. At the same time as the IRB was preparing a rebellion with the support of James Connolly's Irish Citizen Army, so the anonymous Gaelic hero of Loos eulogised from his hospital bed in London about 'the oneness of Empire ... landlord and peasant, Catholic and Protestant, Unionist and Nationalist all friendly as probably never before in Irish history'. Thus establishing that all right thinking Irishmen were now 'vowing vengeance on the Hun', the *Weekly Despatch* stood alone within the context of wider media coverage dampened by the disappointment of Loos rather than the heroism of its 'Irish' participants who led the charge and held the line.

Loos was, and largely remains, essentially a Scottish battle. It was as though the boys of the London Irish had metaphorically dug the ditches and built the roads to watch the parade pass by. They were what Philip Gibbs describes as 'the pawns of strategy', something akin to the Meerut Division of the Indian Corps who charged the enemy lines without sufficient artillery support or any reserves behind them and with no chance of holding any ground they might capture. In order to distract the enemy's attention and hold troops away from the main battlefront, subsidiary attacks were also made upon the German lines north, east and south along the British line in what was essentially a bloody sacrifice. Theirs was not to attract the glory of a victorious assault, but as expendables to soak up the initial heat, which is exactly what they did. Not that the plight of the hapless Indians was in any measure the 'Irish' experience but a parallel is there nevertheless.

59. United Ireland.

The only published account of the London Irish at Loos may well have been instigated by Lord Northcliffe to boost the perception of Ireland as part of Britain's extended family. *The Weekly Despatch* was but one of the many papers and periodicals comprising Northcliffe's Amalgamated Press. *The War Illustrated* was another. The latter's contribution by John Redmond went to huge lengths to demonstrate Ireland's unstinting commitment. The country had always enjoyed a proud military history, he explained. Not always in sympathy with the aims of Empire, but this pride in the past was now more or less a 'secret feeling'. The war had served to fuel the wildest enthusiasm with every record of Irish heroism in the field. On his visit to Irish troops at the Front, Redmond discovered not resentment but 'a message of pride and of gratitude from the whole of the Irish people'. His chief regret was that all the Irish regiments were not combined in distinctively Irish army corps. He would gladly see, for example, the three Irish Divisions of the New Army now at the front combined to form such a corps, but apparently this was held to be 'a military impossibility'.

Then there were the recruiting statistics supplied by the Irish Government, made up to 15 November 1915, which showed when the war commenced there were 20,780 Irishmen in the ranks and in Ireland 12,462 men of the Special Reserve who had since been called up. With 17,804 more reservists and new recruits added, Ireland had with the Colours a total of 138,512 men with thousands more recruited since. All parts of Ireland were represented, Redmond reported, with 82,947 Catholics, 55,565 Protestant with 28,072 members of the National Volunteer Force and 28,327 members of the Ulster Volunteer Force. In considering this 'miracle', it was not sufficient to regard merely the total of recruits drawn from Ireland itself. At least 120,000 men of Irish birth resident in Great Britain had joined the Army since the outbreak of war, which, to Redmond's mind at least, exemplified the transformation of Irish public opinion at home. The same was true of recruits from Canada, Australia, New Zealand and South Africa, where it was estimated that at least 20 per cent were men of Irish birth or Irish blood. All of these were alleged to have been influenced by 'the new wave of friendliness to the Empire which has spread from Ireland right round the world wherever Irishmen are to be found'. 'War is a terrible ordeal for all of us' the Irish leader concluded, finding consolation in the fact that Irish blood was 'being shed willingly in the great cause to seal forever the reconciliation of the two nations'.

In his own patriotic fervour, the anonymous *Weekly Despatch* commentator claimed that the men who kicked the football over the top were professionals who played for the London Irish Football Club. As far as is known, however, this club has only ever played the passing game, the difference between association and rugby football, at that time far more significant as an issue of class when sport was a key player in the emerging political and social Irish landscape.

Although the history of both games in England and Ireland is similar, the appetite for perceived 'English' games was declining in favour of those native to the Emerald Isle. A variety of football games, referred to collectively as 'caid', were once popular in parts of Ireland as either field games or in the true medieval cross-parish manner lasting the whole day and involving vast opposing armies of young men. Although the church had campaigned against the fairs attracting these traditional games in favour of the more organised 'English' ones, the preservation of Irish pastimes was seen as crucial to the cultural reawakening of an Ireland weakened by the effects of British colonialism.

Influenced by hurling and similar to Australian rules football devised in Melbourne in 1858, the first Gaelic Football rules were laid down in 1887 as a specific means of differentiating from Association Football. The only sporting club specifically founded for Irishmen in London was set up in 1898, following the London Welsh in 1895 and the London Scottish in 1878 open to exiles living or working away from home. The founding fathers of the London Irish Football Club comprised politicians, lawyers and businessmen united by a sense of Irishness and a passion for rugby football – not the Association code. The first game was played on 1 October 1898 at Herne Hill Athletic Ground in south-east London, a decent punt from Forest Hill where the *Weekly Despatch* correspondent placed the so-called London Irish 'soccer professionals'. Neither Frank Edwards nor any of his comrades who played the ball towards the German lines was a professional or even a semi-professional footballer. Neither was he, nor were the vast majority of his comrades, Irish.

When the Irish Republican Army was bombing and killing civilians on a daily basis in the 1980s, Prime Minister Margaret Thatcher stated: 'Democratic nations must try to find ways to starve the terrorist and the hijacker of the oxygen of publicity on which they depend.' Publicity, she maintained, gave the IRA what it wanted, an acknowledgment that Britain was at war in Ireland. This was a crucial point for Republicans who sought to legitimise the troubles and forge an historical link between the 1916 insurrection and the later Anglo-Irish war of 1921. Some pundits argued that Thatcher was prompting the mismanagement of truth, as though a problem censored was a problem solved. The draconian guidelines prosecuting the passage of information in 1915 sought to actively celebrate those Irish servants of empire fighting the good cause, which begs the question, why was the London Irish effort at Loos not seized upon both to 'spin' the disappointing outcome of the battle and to further celebrate Irish support?

The *Weekly Despatch* account of the London Irish at Loos reflects the egocentricity of the press baron in an age where wealthy entrepreneurs owned almost 40 per cent of all national newspapers. Since launching the *Daily Mail* in 1896, Lord Northcliffe had by 1908 acquired the *Mirror*, *The Times*, the *Observer* and the *Weekly Despatch*. The 'Northcliffe Revolution,' as it became known, combined the 'popular-educator' emphasis with ruthless marketing. Rather than looking towards improvements in journalism, prominence was given instead to sales-driven, attention-seeking, sensationalist stunts, with advertising as the catalyst. Worse, these notoriously eccentric press barons encouraged the upgrading of popular entertainment at the expense of political analysis.

Beaverbrook, the other prominent newspaper owner, admitted that he used his favourite newspapers purely for propaganda purposes. Northcliffe on the other hand had attacked the government for the debacle at Gallipoli, arguing that even if the campaign had been successful to win the war, the German line on the Western Front had to be broken. The British High Command agreed and so Northcliffe bears some of the responsibility for the small-scale offensives in spring 1915 that eventually made way for the first 'Big Push' at Loos. As well as his vigorous editorial campaigns on the theme of the nation's preparedness, Northcliffe was equally occupied in finding a solution to the omnipresent Irish Question.

The Times, the most powerful organ of opinion for so long hostile to Ireland, had, under Northcliffe's influence, given a sympathetic ear to her sufferings. Born in a small town west of Dublin City, Alfred Harmsworth, later Lord Northcliffe proudly proclaimed himself an 'Irish-born man' with 'a good strain of Irish blood' in him, which drove his belief in Irish settlement and the need for economic and industrial development of the country. In this he shattered a tradition of 'evil association' that for generations had linked *The Times* with unrelenting opposition to Ireland's claim for independence. If the British government had heeded Northcliffe's plea and made 'a supreme effort to find good government for Ireland' all the horrors and manifold disasters after 1916 might have been avoided.

The Times opened its columns to the expression of reasoned opinion on the difficult Irish Question, welcoming discussion of every opinion in the hope of securing some form of appeasement between the opposing factions. It would even institute an independent inquiry of its own, issuing an exhaustive and impartial survey of the entire and hugely complex situation. As with his other campaigns, Northcliffe's pressure on the government would be continuous and consistent, culminating in the summer of 1919 with *The Times* publishing its own plan of settlement that would be used to form the basis for the Government of Ireland Act. What appeared in the *Weekly Despatch* four years earlier was no official report on the Battle of Loos. It was a populist effort based on available information used to arouse sympathy for an Ireland on the verge of revolution and anarchy. A total and complete disunion with a Britain at war with the deadliest foes she had faced since the threat of Napoleon would, and eventually did see after Easter 1916, any public sympathy turn to anger and retribution. Whether or not the anonymous rifleman who regaled *Despatch* readers with his eyewitness account of Loos actually existed is beside the point. What he did and did not see or personally experience is largely irrelevant. Where Northcliffe wanted his popular readership to empathise was in the language of a good and true Irish boy, ready to put any personal grievance to one side, as proud to have fought for King and country as any other servant of Empire.

Studies of the 'Irish experience' during the First World War are rare. One comprehensive study examining questions of motivation, loyalty and allegiance is Timothy Bowman's *Irish Regiments in the Great War – Discipline and Morale*, published in 2003. In it, the 10th (Irish), the 16th (Irish) and the 36th (Ulster) Divisions are examined to evaluate Irish discipline and morale using the courts martial records released in 1995. The 330 records proved extremely limited, however, presenting only problems of morale with more convictions in Irish units for drunkenness, serious indiscipline and a higher incidence of mutiny. Of these, just ten per cent of the trial transcripts survive and then only for capital cases where the sentence was carried out. While it is shown that the regular soldier was more prone to these misdemeanours than volunteers, there is no context for the political situation in Ireland which prevented the rise of the New Army volunteer movement like that on the mainland.

The differences between Irish and other units of the British Army appear founded on the individual experiences of errant English, Scottish or Welsh soldiers who were more likely to appear before their commanding officer, unlike their Irish counterparts who were more often tried by court martial and mostly sentenced to short terms of field punishment. Bowman also found that Irish allegiance was invariably to regiment rather than region, ethnicity or nationalism and that the court martial record was different for each of the 56 infantry battalions and six cavalry regiments examined. Overall, it appears that even during the so-called 'crisis periods' towards the 1916 Uprising, Sinn Fein made little attempt to subvert Irish soldiers, regarding those serving in the British Army already lost to the cause. These records of performance were dependent on the guiding principles of commanders, an element not necessarily confined to Irish regiments. The London Irish Rifles was a London Territorial battalion formed originally of the Irish immigrant population. Its value in terms of pro-Irish cant was limited by the perceived failure of Loos and a truth determined by the state.

Edmund Burke is often credited with coining of the term 'The Fourth Estate' thanks to a citation by historian Thomas Carlyle in *Heroes and Hero-Worship* written in 1839. Carlyle states: 'Burke said that there were three estates in Parliament; but, in the Reporters' Gallery yonder, there sat a Fourth Estate more important by far than them all'. Other observers believe that

Carlyle was referring to Lord Macaulay, who said in 1828 that the gallery in which the reporters sit 'has become a Fourth Estate of the realm'. Among other contenders for the expression, the Oxford English Dictionary suggests Lord Brougham first applied it to the Press in the House of Commons in 1823. Whatever its precise root, the sentiment remains the same to this day in that it is the press that seeds much of popular perception in what it chooses to report and the manner in which it so does. A good story will always out irrespective of the facts.

Chapter Ten

Press and Propaganda

Whereas it was the readership that fuelled the newspaper interest in the 1914 Christmas Truce, so the authorities allowed Billie Nevill's act of bravado to sweeten the bitter pill of the Somme eighteen months later. Frank Edwards' audacity midway never entered the popular psyche because Loos was a story in need of burial. Overall, the promotion of biased or deliberately mislead-ing information was used extensively from the start of the war to encourage recruitment and to maintain morale. Information coming from the Front was censored to ensure a constant flow of positive news.

As early as 1909 the newspaper magnate, Lord Northcliffe, vehemently main-tained that Germany was deliberately preparing to destroy the British Empire. He issued warnings in a series of articles urging Britain to spend more money on defence or face the danger of being defeated in a war. The *Star* claimed that next to the Kaiser, Northcliffe, in his consistent attacks on the government for its many shortfalls, had done more than any living man to bring about the conflict. The enthusiasm expressed in *The Times*, the *Daily Mail* and other Northcliffe newspapers over the eventual decision to go to war with Germany was by no means universal. Several other prominent papers such as the *Manchester Guardian* and the *Daily News* were against it, which forced the government to set up its Parliamentary War Aims Committee to propagate material for pro-war papers such as those owned by Northcliffe in the belief that a concerted propa-ganda campaign would weaken the German spirit and raise British morale at home. Stories of German atrocities thereafter were legion, although the sala-cious tales of mass rape and other unspeakable violations daily taking up British and French column inches were invariably entire fiction put about mostly by Britain's other foremost newspaper proprietor, Lord Beaverbrook.

In putting to one side the egocentricities of these powerful press barons, it was David Lloyd George, as Chancellor of the Exchequer, who set about the task of gearing up a propaganda agency like that already in place in Germany. With the Defence of the Realm Act (DORA) in place to ensure government control over information, the writer and fellow Liberal MP, Charles Masterman, was appointed as head of the War Propaganda Bureau (WPB) who in turn invited a series of leading British artists and authors to promote Britain's interests during the conflict. Much of the recruitment art used the relationship between sport and war to urge men to 'join the team' and to 'play the game'. Terms such as 'good hunting' were widely used to make light of killing or to emphasize the virtues of good sportsmanship akin to patriotism. In February 1915 the great Dutch illustrator, Louis Raemakers, provided the highly disconcerting illustrations in one of the first WPB pamphlets reporting on alleged German outrages, which attempted to give credence to the idea of the 'evil Hun' systematically torturing civilians. From May 1916 to 1917 a small army of celebrated artists were sent to France and produced thousands of drawings and paintings of the war. Later, Lord Beaverbrook, as Minister of Information, rapidly expanded their number, establishing with Arnold Bennett a British War Memorial Committee (BWMC) with the aim of no longer primarily contributing to propaganda, but producing pictures as a matter of record. Of the ninety or so artists producing work for the government during the war, some produced very little, while others complained about the government's control over subject matter.

Charles Masterman invited 25 leading British authors to discuss ways of best promoting Britain's interests during the war. Those attending included Arthur Conan Doyle, Arnold Bennett, John Masefield, G. K. Chesterton, Sir Henry Newbolt, John Galsworthy, Thomas Hardy, Rudyard Kipling, and H. G. Wells. All those who agreed to write pamphlets and books aimed at promoting the government line were bound to the utmost secrecy, as were the major publishing houses such as Hodder & Stoughton, Methuen, Oxford University Press, John Murray, Macmillan and Thomas Nelson who agreed to print the material. As well as 1,160 pamphlets published by the WPB during the war, was a history of the war in the form of a monthly magazine. In this, Masterman recruited John Buchan, using his own publishing company, Thomas Nelson, to produce *Nelson's History of the War*. The first edition appeared in February 1915 and was followed by a further 23 editions at regular intervals throughout the war. Buchan was given the rank of Second Lieutenant in the Intelligence Corps and was provided with the documents needed to write the accounts. However, his close relationships with the military leaders made it very difficult for him to include any critical comments about the way the war was being fought. Also, only two official photographers, both army officers, were allowed to take the right sort of pictures that would help the war effort. The penalty for anyone else caught photographing the war was the firing squad.

No sooner was the British Expeditionary Force in action than Lord Northcliffe looked to make the *Daily Mail* the official newspaper of the British Army, arranging for 10,000 copies of the paper to be delivered daily to troops on the Western Front using military transport. While in French territory in 1915, Captain C. J. C. Street came across a bearded French solider who he imagined was a news vendor in civilian life because in his free time he would walk many miles and return with an armful of day-old English newspapers. How he procured them no one knew, as he always arrived with them days before they were delivered officially and at a reduced price. 'Dele Peppers!' he would cry out and always knew the contents of the papers he sold, especially the *Daily Mail* whose proprietor, Lord Northcliffe he thought was either the Dictator of England or had changed places with Lord Kitchener.

As early as August 1914 Northcliffe had already floated the revolutionary idea of using frontline soldiers as news sources and announced a scheme whereby they would be paid for articles written about their experiences. Instead, the War Office Press Bureau was established to censor news and reports from the British Army before issuing it to the press. Even with this machinery in place, all news from the Western Front prior to publication had to be cleared with Lord Kitchener, the Secretary of State for War. Any bad news was filtered out, with the threat of imprisonment without trial under DORA for newspaper editors failing to spread the word that the government wanted the public to hear. Letters home from troops at the front were also heavily censored. As well as a ban on giving information about military positions or battles, soldiers were not allowed to describe the true nature of the appalling conditions in which they were living and dying. Postcards pre-printed with a list of statements to be ticked where appropriate ensured that nothing negative could be communicated, including if the writer was injured. Thus the British government and military leaders maintained total control over the actual casualties and conditions.

Ernest Swinton was appointed by Lord Kitchener to become the British Army's official journalist on the Western Front. Using the pseudonym, 'Eyewitness', his articles were initially censored at General Headquarters in France and then personally vetted by Kitchener before release to the press. *Daily News* journalist, Henry Major Tomlinson, was also recruited as an official war correspondent, working with Swinton to strict guidelines. These correspondents were not allowed to mention place names, battalions, brigades or divisions and no article would be passed for publication if it indicated that a reporter had witnessed events for himself and in terms of what he believed rather than what he knew to be true. Given all of this, the *Weekly Despatch* account of the London Irish at Loos is in clear contravention of these regulations, although as far as is known no action appears to have been taken against the paper or its proprietor, Lord Northcliffe. From the start of the conflict Northcliffe had courted massive controversy advocating by conscription and in his blistering criticisms of Lord Kitchener. In an article he wrote on 21 May 1915, Northcliffe claimed that Kitchener was starving the Army in France of the high-explosive shells it desperately needed and that those being used were of the wrong kind. Kitchener was a national hero and Northcliffe's attacks were deeply unpopular, sending the circulation of the *Daily Mail* plummeting overnight from well over 1,000,000 copies to fewer than 300,000. Unabashed Northcliffe's newspaper campaigns continued and were a determining factor in Britain's conduct of the war.

Kitchener's initial ban on newspaper correspondents going to the Front gave Germany the edge over a neutral United States in the propaganda war and so after complaints from the Americans, the British government reviewed the situation. Following a Cabinet meeting in January 1915 it decided on a change of policy that would allow five journalists to report on the war. These were Philip Gibbs of the *Daily Chronicle* and *Daily Telegraph*, Percival Philips of the *Daily Express* and the *Morning Post*, the *Daily Mail* and *Daily Mirror's* William Beach Thomas, Henry Perry Robinson of *The Times* and *Daily News*, and Reuters' Herbert Russell. C. E. Montague – the former leader writer of the *Manchester Guardian* – was charged with vetting each report before it was passed back to England. Over the next three years John Buchan would join Valentine Williams, Hamilton Fyfe and Henry Nevinson in the ranks of accredited war correspondents, still subject to strict government control. As a result, and with the connivance of the press, blunders were covered up and German victories ignored. In the early days of the war at least, any attempt by journalists other than to lend themselves to the integrity and credibility of the propaganda would have at best been disbelieved by the public and at worst led to their arrest. *The History of the War* monthly, for example, was wildly over-optimistic in its reporting of the events on the Western Front, claiming in 1915 that the Germans were on the verge of defeat with an estimated loss of over 1,300,000 men compared to a loss of 'only' 100,000 British lives.

Between the autumn of 1914 and the following summer, the French had fought numerous small offensive actions, suffering heavy losses and failing to make any strategic impact on the continued German possession. With sufficient numbers of British troops in place, the Allies were eager to make inroads into the German lines. Northcliffe's constant campaigning, centred on his belief that the time was right for the British Army to push the Germans back, was consistent with the view of the Allied commander-in-chief, Joseph Joffre, who, despite severe reservations expressed by British generals, determined the action at Loos.

The front page of the 27 September 1915 edition of the *London Evening News* (another Northcliffe paper) succinctly set out Sir John French's despatch from

General Headquarters announcing that the Battle of Loos had taken place. Above this meagre bulletin was an imposing 'special sketch' of the Allied commander-in-chief, '*Grandpere*' Joseph Joffre, the man who had engineered the 'Big Push'.

In his report for Northcliffe's *Daily Mail* two days after the initial attack, Valentine Williams maintained that it was too soon to write in any detail about the battle, as the fighting was still in progress. Instead he turned to German prisoners and learned from them that the attack by the British had taken them completely by surprise. This was despite known intelligence and the most intensive artillery bombardment of the war to date, specifically designed to soften up the German defences. The artillery bombardment was described as 'unspeakable' by captured troops. The rolling cloud of smoke and gas appeared to have somehow passed the enemy by, or was such an insignificant event that it did not warrant a mention. The German prisoners claimed that had their ammunition not run out they 'might not have felt obliged to surrender'.

The day after the initial assault, the *London Gazette* reported that the king was pleased to award the Victoria Cross to Lance-Sergeant Oliver Brooks of the 3rd Battalion, Coldstream Guards, for most conspicuous bravery near Loos when he led a party of bombers in regaining possession of lost ground. Four days later and the London Irish Rifles were afforded a coded mention as a 'certain battalion' that had led the charge. On 9 October, three days before the end of the first Great Push on the Western Front, the *Illustrated London News* published one of its splendid centrepiece sketches by artist Samuel Begg showing men of a Scottish regiment charging over German trenches during the battle. Another illustration in that same magazine a week later once again depicted the Scots before the attack preparing a telephone line under fire in a forward trench. In the background looms large the outstanding feature on the landscape, the pithead composed of two steel latticework towers joined by a similarly constructed gantry near their summit. Inevitably the structure was nicknamed Tower Bridge by men of the London Regiment whose presence went entirely unrecorded.

These 'London Territorials', as they were later described, did eventually make the pages of the popular illustrated paper, pictured complete with their weird gas hoods and long rifles attacking the German lines with bombs and bayonets. The caption beneath bizarrely came from a German reporter on *Berliner Tageblatt* describing the unidentified 'hooded familiars of the Inquisition' as 'not like soldiers, but like devils'. These dramatic depictions, emblematic of the *Illustrated London News* and *The War Illustrated*, were produced in cooperation with officers who took part in the action, or at least those who survived and had some knowledge of the events. Clearly there was no such witness on hand to record the actions of the London Irish Rifles. For all its colour and

60. General Joffre.

heightened drama, *The Weekly Despatch* stood alone as the single commentary, as well as offering a genuine taste of life and death experienced at the Front and an idea of what ordinary men were doing and thinking. For the most part each edition of the *Illustrated London News* marked en masse the anonymity of the thousands of such men killed in action, reserving two full pages for the names and faces of officers 'dead on the field of honour'. They were as much victims of an incompetent hierarchy as were the hundreds of thousands of others who went obediently and meekly to their deaths at their command. But just as Kitchener's press and propaganda machine sought to disguise this ineptitude, so deference would gradually die on the killing fields of France and elsewhere. The 'unenlightened and unimaginative censorship' exercised by the Army's senior commanders, could not and would not be entirely contained.

★ ★ ★

Press and Propaganda

On leave and walking up Villiers Street to the Strand, Henry Williamson's Phillip Maddison comes across a paper boy crying out: 'New attack on Western Front! Loos battle flares up!' Maddison buys a *Star* and reads the brief communiqué from GHQ declaring the morale of British troops to be excellent, which was something that 'belonged to the scene all around him, of the world beyond the pallor of the flares which he had forsaken'. In his book, *With The Guns*, Captain C. J. C. Street writes of the 'fatal delay, which left the attacking divisions unsupported and checked an advance', which may well have resulted in the capture of Lens and sealed the fate of Lille. Street also supports the claims of captured enemy prisoners in that they anticipated the worst in the early hours of the morning, but that 'the feebleness of the final blow amazed them'. From a gunner's perspective the order to lift fire onto a more distant point early in the action seemed to indicate that the attack was forging ahead. But then, almost immediately, fire was directed back on to a point thought to have been captured long ago, bringing the brief euphoria of the gunners crashing down. All the while the road was filling with an ever-increasing flow of ambulances laden with stretchers and other casualties less severely wounded supporting one another as best they could. 'I think that none of us realised till we saw the magnitude of this stream, how fierce a fight was raging in front of us' writes Street.

As soon as Loos was taken, the enemy opened up a steady artillery barrage upon the village in order to prevent its use by the British gunners for further attack and to hinder observation from the various landmarks it contained. With so little natural cover, Street saw this as a serious disadvantage. The communication trenches leading from the British-held German front line were choked with dead, and reinforcements had to run a gauntlet of heavy fire in order to reach the line of attack. Street writes openly in 1916 of the greatest slaughter at Loos taking place on the Lens-Bethune road where an entire divisional train was overwhelmed by shrapnel, blocking the road for a quarter of a mile with shattered wagons and dead horses. Street identifies a photograph of this debris that subsequently did the rounds of the illustrated press under the more uplifting heading of 'Captured German Battery at Loos'. Two British field batteries that attempted to come into action in the open between Quality Street and La Chapelle de Notre Dame de Consolation suffered heavily and were silenced. 'Of the losses of the infantry' Street laments, 'nobody who did not see the procession of casualties and, worse still, the burial parties of the next few days, can form an adequate picture.' Reading of the British offensive in the west, and the gain of five miles of trench, Captain Street records that 'each foot of that five miles cost us a life and a sum of human agony such as this world has never known'.

In 1978, journalists William Allison and John Fairley revisited the six-day mutiny at Etaples army camp in 1917 and the role played by Percy Toplis, or

61. Men of Sportsmen's Battalion reading *The War Illustrated*.

The Monocled Mutineer as he became better known from the subsequent BBC television series. Allison and Fairley claim that the authorities tried to dismiss the fact that the uprising – said to have involved thousands of troops – ever took place. Central to the story is Percy Toplis, a confidence trickster who crossed the boundaries of place by cocking a snoop at the officer class and in turn ridiculing the entire establishment. A figurehead reactionary in a war that would change the British way of life forever, he was ultimately blamed for the mutiny. Seventy years later and the BBC was demonised for transmitting the story. Its director general at the time, Alasdair Milne, was made scapegoat in the face of malevolent right-wing press criticism aligned to a government determined to bring down what it perceived to be a reactionary, left-wing and ill-disciplined state broadcaster.

Of all the propagandist organs circulating non-facts and misinformation about the management of the First World War, it is *The War Illustrated* that best and most consistently exemplifies the level of sanitation maintained by the authorities as a matter of public record, deviating only to doff its hat to the awkward issue of fraternisation during the first Christmas of the war. Two weeks after the event it published what it called 'pictorial proof of the Christmas Day Truce', showing British and German 'friends' posing for the camera, explaining in the brief caption that such an incident was not uncommon in warfare and had occurred during the Napoleonic and Russo-Japanese campaigns. In the 1915 Christmas edition the paper explained that the 'rapprochement' which took place was 'a great scandal', but understandable given that the Saxon soldiers 'represented the very best of the German army', who throughout had been 'noted for their humanity' and therefore 'most nearly resembled our lads'. But things had changed. Too many bitter recriminations had passed over the previous twelve months for such an incident to re-occur, not least the shocking treatment of captured and wounded troops – and the German use of poison gas. Arguably the most obtuse citation littering this rag invited readers to peruse a selection of 'New Year Novelties' to be found in the trenches of what it headlined the 'Ever-Wonderful War'.

★ ★ ★

In mid-September 1915, F. A. McKenzie, *The War Illustrated's* own correspondent, stood at a point on the British Front in Flanders where he was able to inspect a long stretch of the German lines. They ran back in irregular threefold formation, he reported, each section connected with the other by numerous shelter and communicating trenches. Behind them were hidden guns, 'spitting out their afternoon hate at us'. These lines were formidable. 'To a layman they might have seemed impregnable' but McKenzie knew something of the deep German trenches, the stores of bombs, the mortars, the mines, and, he claimed, the poison gas. 'Come and touch us if you dare' was the challenge written all over the stout German defences. By McKenzie's side stood a British officer pointing to the heart of the German position, believing that in three weeks the Hun would be pushed out. But he was wrong. British troops would be there with a week to spare. 'The Great Push', as McKenzie described it had come at last, the weeks waiting were worth it. Ahead lay the first great triumph since the Marne, which, if carried to the point he hoped, would surpass in importance even that battle that had saved Paris and the coast. This big advance was ending the stalemate and giving the Allies the key to the heart of the German position in France and in Western Flanders.

On the morning of 29 September, McKenzie wrote: 'much will happen before these words can be published. The point was yet to be reached as to who would be the victor.' But Loos, he observed, had proved that it was possible to break through the strongest German defences. Thousands of prisoners had been captured and many guns. The quality of the artillery had been proved, but there was no need to prove the spirit of the men. While a decision as to the actual outcome of the battle was yet to be reached, in examining what happened there was every cause for hope, confidence and rejoicing, he claimed, reflecting on Ypres which had proved 'a horrible disappointment' despite the Germans' inability to break through. The main cause of the Allied defeat there, he explained, was the lack of high-explosive shells, which created a bitter outcry back home fuelled by his boss, Lord Northcliffe, who had fanned the flames of discontent which saw defences strengthened, additional men deployed and stocks of shells and machine-guns increased. Now, complete with weapons equalling in effectiveness anything the Germans could muster, it was reported, the campaign opened at the beginning of September. Heavy artillery duels at numerous points along the land front were so overwhelming as to puzzle the Germans where the strike would come from. There was good reason to believe, according to McKenzie, that the Germans no longer employed the same manpower on the Western Front as they once had. The Russian campaign was taking its toll and it was 'a well-known principle of the German Army' to employ old men for the tedium of the trenches, while keeping the younger, fitter troops in reserve.

Captain C. J. C. Street, however, again disagrees. In his 'sketchbook' of Loos, he is clear that the enemy was well aware of their strengths and weaknesses based on a strategy to concentrate their forces on the edge of the valley, leaving sufficient strengths over losses not to outweigh the gains of the main defence. One battery in position along the Loos-Benifontaine road remained in action against huge odds until the last man fell. 'Let us give the enemy his due' Street observes, making it clear that the Allies were not fighting a nation of cowards and assassins, 'as we are so fond of trying to believe', but brave and determined men, difficult to defeat. The few hundred German prisoners marched past Street's battery to the rear included

> … fine upstanding men enough, looking perfectly fit and in the prime of life, disposing effectually, in my mind at least, of the fable born of our national love for self-deceit that the enemy were hard put to it to find men fit for service.

F. A. McKenzie makes no mention of the use of poison gas by the British. Instead the reader's main focus of attention is directed to the detonation of explosives piled up in a tunnel dug under the German lines, which he claimed was the signal for the advance. Of many a tale told of heroism following in the wake of the charge, McKenzie chose the capture of prisoners and guns, as 'already the stuff of legend'. He reported the Germans bringing up their reserves but not the British failure to do likewise, but then Loos was only the start. The aim of the Allies was to rid France and Belgium of the German invader before the second winter. Great things would happen 'once the cavalry was let lose behind the German lines' and so it was unwise to harbour any 'foolish optimism' over the ultimate effects of the advance at Loos. Even if it turned out to be a magnificent victory, it would not end the war. It was the prelude to a long, fierce campaign requiring more and more men for an assault made on an even grander scale that would result in final triumph.

A few weeks later, however, and *The War Illustrated* adapted its view. 'The Memorable Capture of Loos' was now officially assigned one of 'The Great Episodes of the War', its passage marking a positive stage in the progress of the conflict. Readers were told that for months the German High Command had been fooled into believing that it would be impossible for the Allies to breach their lines 'of steel and fire'. The advance on Loos and the French success in Champagne had proved that assumption wrong. The magazine maintained that no one below Allied general staff knew of the plan until the eve of the attack. While the London Territorials chosen to lead the charge were not mentioned, the great expectations of the Guards Division held in reserve were fulsomely recorded. McKenzie had already reported on the greatest artillery bombardment of the war to date, yet a reader new to the story would believe that only 'the German guns were busy'. The failure of the British guns to decimate the enemy lines as planned may have had morale implications, but in quite the most blatant piece of dishonest misreporting, *The War Illustrated* representative told of how the enemy had released 'their reserve weapon – poison gas'.

In its own tempered supplement, the *London Gazette* reported on the 'London Territorial Division' acquitting itself

… most creditably in the taking of Loos. Skillfully led and with the troops carrying out their task with great energy and determination, they contributed largely to our success in this part of the field.

The magazine published details of individuals who had shown exceptional acts of heroism, gallantry and devotion to duty, such as acting Second Corporal A. Adamson, 3rd Field Squadron, Royal Engineers, who delivered two carts under heavy rifle and shrapnel fire, Lance-Corporal J. Aitken of the 1st Battalion, Scots Guards who carried his severely injured Company Officer 400 yards under heavy fire to a place of safety. Private T. Allan of the 10th Battalion, Gordon Highlanders, who carried messages to and from the firing line under heavy fire continuously for 24 hours, assisted in bringing up ammunition, led a large party of men through Loos to Hill 70 and carried from it a wounded officer under very heavy fire. Other papers and periodicals carried the stirring account of Piper Daniel Laidlaw of the King's Own Scottish Borderers, who roused the men disorientated by the gas carried back into the Scots' own front-line. He continued playing throughout, oblivious to his own safety and was later awarded the Victoria Cross and the French Croix de Guerre and promoted to corporal for his action at Loos.

The War Illustrated carried the splendid illustration of a latter day Joan of Arc caught up in the advance units of the 15th (Scottish) Division fighting their way through the German lines and into the village of Loos. In order to cope

62. The Piper of Loos.

with the rapidly increasing casualties, a dressing-station was set up among the ruined buildings where seventeen-year-old Emilienne Moreau fought side by side with the British soldiers as she tended the wounded. Killing five Germans with a revolver and grenades, she was awarded the Military Medal and the Croix de Guerre.

The men of the London Territorials were not entirely unrepresented. Adding to the roll call of heroes in a full-page action scene, *The War Illustrated* featured one of its own employees, Private F. G. Challoner, 6th (City of London) Battalion, London Regiment (T.F), who was awarded the Distinguished Conduct Medal for conspicuous gallantry in action at Loos. Far ahead of his comrades, Private Challoner charged the enemy first-line trench in face of withering shell, machine-gun and rifle-fire. Jumping down into a crowded trench, he shot and bayoneted nine Germans. So inspired were his comrades, that they charged the remaining German trenches again and again until they broke through.

The pre-Christmas edition of *The War Illustrated* carried a special supplement panorama depicting the successful charge at Loos painted by Stanley L. Wood. Pre-eminent in the ranks are mad-eyed Scots storming the German ramparts. The successful route of the German second trench by the London Irish went unrecorded and unrecognised. But the footballing episode was not entirely ignored. The late October edition of *The War Illustrated* did carry the full page illustration of the gallant officer scoring a goal on the field of war, a 'proverbial sporting spirit of the Britons on the battlefield'. It must have been galling for Frank Edwards to see himself depicted thus, also reading also of how, shortly after kicking off the ball, he was struck down.

Perhaps for these reasons it was down to the *Weekly Despatch* to put the record straight, or at least provide the closest account of the facts surrounding the new Regiment's assault and stand at Loos. Curiously, *The Weekly Despatch* shared the same stable as *The War Illustrated*. The latter very much played the game. The *Despatch* on this occasion reported very much from a personal point of view how the war was going, what the men were thinking and essentially how the mightiest and most concerted artillery barrage to date had failed in its objective. It made plain that it was the British who had sent poison gas rolling across No Man's Land and not the Germans. It also detailed how the London Irish held the line until the reserves finally arrived.

Such an apparently arbitrary decision to deviate from the stated principles of censorship could not have been made by Spencer Brodney, the editor of the *Weekly Despatch*. In so doing he would have effectively delivered a broadside at J. A. Hammerton, his colleague at Amalgamated Press and editor of *The War Illustrated*. Only Northcliffe himself could have sanctioned such a profound departure. Perhaps he empathised with grievances expressed by troops at the Front or possibly it was another opportunity to take a swipe at Kitchener – there was no love lost between the two. As much as Northcliffe used the power of his press to embarrass the Secretary of State for War, so did the latter harbour nothing but contempt for 'newspaper fellows who defied all orders'. Had the decision been made by Brodney to report Loos in his publication in the way that it did then in all probability he may have found himself in prison. Indeed, Kitchener once had the journalist Philip Gibbs arrested on reaching the port of Le Harve, considering him a particularly 'loose-lipped nuisance and a potential hazard'. The base commander at Le Havre, General Bruce Williams, shared Kitchener's disdain for those he considered were spending the war smuggling back 'uncensored nonsense'. After nearly a fortnight under close arrest in a local hotel, Gibbs managed to get a letter back to Robert Donald, the editor of the *Daily Chronicle*, explaining his plight. After a call to a contact at the Foreign Office, Gibbs was allowed to return to England.

Despite Kitchener's personal animosity towards him, Gibbs was eventually appointed one of only five reporters accredited as official war correspondents with the British Armies in the Field. The relationship was sour too between Gibbs and Sir Douglas Haig who also harboured an extreme prejudice against war correspondents and other 'writing fellows'. When he became commander-in-chief, Haig told the small corps of journalists that they were only writing for 'Mary Ann in the kitchen', to which Gibbs retorted that they were writing for the whole nation and the Empire. Moreover he told Haig he could not expect to be able to conduct his war in secret, 'as though the people at home, whose sons and husbands were fighting and dying, had no concern in the matter'.

Philip Gibbs was one of a number of top-flight journalists recruited by Robert Donald who took charge as editor of the *Daily Chronicle* in 1904. Building on its high reputation, Donald increased its circulation, transforming the paper into a halfpenny daily. By 1914, the net sales of the *Chronicle* were said to have exceeded the combined sales of *The Times*, *Daily Telegraph*, *Morning Post*, *Evening Standard* and the *Daily Graphic*. At the end of July 1914 when it became clear that Britain was on the verge of war with Germany, the *Chronicle*, as a supporter of the left-wing Liberal Party, sympathised with those members of the government opposed to war. Unlike his Liberal peers, David Lloyd George did not resign from the government but managed to persuade Robert Donald to give the *Daily Chronicle* its full support to the war effort, which he did. In his reports for the paper, Gibbs was often highly critical of those in command. He believed that the guiding idea behind the censorship was not to conceal the truth from the enemy, but from the nation in defence of the British high command and its tragic blundering.

Gibbs's take on Loos was as 'a ghastly failure after the first smash through'. The facts were clear for all to see. The two fresh divisions of reserves were held too far back and came up too late. When they did arrive they had no maps, no topographical intelligence and generally 'made an awful mess of things' – but through no fault of their own. The forward line under huge pressure, having received no support at the right time, lacked the strength to resist counter-attacks. Thus Gibbs was summoned to have breakfast at Downing Street with Lloyd George where he was asked by the Prime Minister to tell him first hand what he knew about the Battle of Loos. In an extraordinary admission, Lloyd George told the journalist:

> I am a Cabinet Minister, but we know nothing. Everything is held back from us by the military chiefs, and we have a right to know. How can we conduct this war if we are kept in ignorance?

Gibbs made no comment. Much to the Prime Minister's distress, he told Lloyd George what he knew.

Philip Gibbs later refuted the notion that the First World War correspondents were spoon fed stories. He maintained that it was decided among the reporters themselves to pool all information received in order to give the fullest record of any action, with only personal impressions and experiences reserved for individual use. While they each understood the need to hide the numbers of casualties from the enemy, their worst handicap was in the prohibition of naming individual units who had done the fighting. Like the generals, not

63. Lloyd George.

all journalists covering the First World War were incompetent or weighed down with misguided patriotism or subservience to a government agenda. It is debateable who first coined the phrase 'the first casualty of war is the truth'. According to Northcliffe, 'the truth is what someone else didn't want you to know, everything else is advertising'.

In February 1917 the Department of Information was established, with John Buchan given the rank of lieutenant colonel. This was the man who had written the pamphlet, *The Battle of the Somme*, in which the British Army's blackest day is spun as 'so successful' that it marked 'the end of trench fighting and the beginning of the campaign in the open'. Charles Masterman retained responsibility for books, pamphlets, photographs and war paintings, and T. L. Gilmour for cables, wireless, newspapers, magazines and the cinema. A year later, the view was taken that a senior government figure should take over responsibility for propaganda, and Lord Beaverbrook was chosen as Minister of Information. Masterman reported to him as Director of Publications and Buchan as Director of Intelligence. Lord Northcliffe was tasked with presiding over all propaganda directed at enemy countries, and Robert Donald was appointed Director of Propaganda in neutral countries. In this, David Lloyd

George was heavily criticised in the House of Commons for engineering a system effectively controlling the leading press barons. It was only Northcliffe's *Weekly Despatch* that reported in detail the London Irish effort at Loos, using the footballing episode as an example of mankind's indomitable spirit over disaster. And it was Northcliffe's *Evening News* that maintained interest in the story right up until 1964 when Frank Edwards died. Even so, when the first histories of the battle came to be written, it was still the censors and Maude's terse legacy in his history of the 47th Division that held sway.

Chapter Eleven

Conclusions

The History of the 47th (London) Division 1914–1919 was published in 1922. Its editor, Alan H. Maude, pays tribute to 'the many hands' that contributed to its production by way of official war diaries and personal narratives. In the accepted manner, an officer either in command of a battalion, or with special knowledge of a specific operation, helped compile each chapter. Proofs were submitted to units and to numerous members of the Division for corrections and additions. Understandably, Maude states, it was impossible to include every act of special distinction and individual gallantry. Also, that it was important to 'secure accuracy and completeness with which to provide a proper perspective relative to each particular operation'. On the one hand, Maude mildly begrudges the paucity of press coverage at the time with regard to the Division's achievements at Loos, while on the other he admonishes those accounts that managed to evade the censor. The Division's place in history, he advocates, rests on Loos being the first large scale use of the New Army where the success of the attack was founded on an operation carried out to clearly defined objectives. He does, however, express disappointment that the Division failed to enjoy 'the main share of prisoners and spoils of war' that it deserved. Had Sir John French delivered the reserves as was planned, then the attackers would not have been bogged down for days awaiting their arrival.

Maude records that of those who took part in the actual attack, the 141st Brigade had furthest to go. It was led by the 1st Battalion London Irish Rifles, whose objective was the German second line from the Lens-Bethune road to Loos cemetery. Comparatively speaking, No Man's Land proved easy going, unlike the German first line where the difficulties began, and not the second as expected. This notwithstanding, the second line was reached well within time. Within the overall context of each individual engagement taking place, Maude admits that it was not possible to assess the value of the work of each division.

In *The History of the 47th (London) Division*, as elsewhere, it is the valour of other battalions comprising 141st Brigade generally and the Scottish divisions in particular that are best recorded. In the inevitable confusion of battle, the actual position of 47th Division and 141st Brigade is not officially clear, although General Thwaites did hold the least stable portion of the line, and all his battalions had fought hard for the ground they had made and against all odds retained it. His left flank was unprotected except by actions on open ground between Loos and Hulluch, which was going in favour of the enemy. The withdrawal of the 15th Division had left a gap of about a mile between the left of 141st Brigade and the 1st near Hulluch. The 47th's line from the spinney to the Loos Crassier was held by the 17th and 20th Battalions, but to the north the village lay open to attack. In support, just west of the village was the 18th Battalion, which, early in the afternoon of the 23rd was sent forward to maintain the second line northwards to the Loos–Vermelles road. The west of the spinney was still in German hands and which took the repeated demands of Thwaites for heavy artillery support before he could launch an attack.

All that stated, Maude claims that in retrospect it was impossible to follow the course of all the actions, and there's the rub. Rumours and reports were coming in ad infinitum and from all quarters. Small bodies of men and individuals had conflicting stories, mostly of disaster or defeat. Thwaites meanwhile remained steadfast and his position is clear. He ordered his COs to impress on their officers and men that they were to hold their positions at all costs. He moved his advanced HQ from Le Maroc to a much more hazardous location where at night contact with Divisional Headquarters by telegraph proved impossible as the least glimmer of light would have signalled a heavy artillery barrage. In such circumstances and 'only by constant effort' the 47th maintained its position day and night without respite, exactly as the anonymous London Irish Rifleman would later disclose to readers of the *Weekly Despatch*. With the eventual capture of the spinney representing the last objective of Thwaites' Brigade, so the reserves eventually arrived. Thus, the advance of the 3rd Guards Brigade on Hill 70 and the Welsh Guards, in action for the time, entered the Loos record. On the night of 29/30 September 142nd Brigade relieved the 141st, who 'after four days spent in the most critical part of the divisional front' were withdrawn in to reserve at Le Maroc to fade into the footnotes of First World War history. Maude records Sir John French inspecting the 142nd Brigade, chosen to represent the Division and to them he expressed 'in his strongest terms' an appreciation of the value of the Division's performance, 'the success of which, had definitely assured him of the safety of the most vulnerable point in the field of operations'. The 142nd Brigade was not intended for use in the first phases of the attack. Instead it held the line for the Division while the other brigades rehearsed and rested. It was relieved during the night of 24 September.

Maude offers no opinion, his view being that popular fancy was most impressed by the use of the New Army first employed on a large scale. Beyond that, his preference lay with the Kitchener school of reportage over that 'apt to give most scope to the imagination of the war correspondent'. The 47th had a job to do with clearly defined objectives, which it did and saw through as was expected of it. That the main glory was distributed elsewhere was unfortunate but understandable. The 47th performed a distinct and important function in the general scheme. It was 'the hinge upon which the attack swung'. Once captured and the position held, Maude admits, the hardest part 'is not in rest, but work and defence against all comers'.

Irrespective of individual opinion, the facts of the matter surrounding the Battle of Loos are that it was the first 'Big Push' by British troops into German-held territory where more than 61,000 casualties were sustained, of which 7,766 died. Casualties were particularly high among the Scots, with many of the New Army units rushed into battle for the first time, some a matter of days after landing in France. A significant proportion of the surviving British Army regulars were lost, and more than 2,000 officers were killed or wounded. Loos was the principal British effort that only fell short of victory because the reserves were not made available to follow up the initial success.

As well as these factors, Loos' place in history was further marginalised by a horse when King George V travelled to France to determine whether or not Sir John French should retain command of the main British Front. The king was lent a flighty mare from Haig's personal stable to ride during an inspection. Sir Douglas Haig wasted no time in fuelling discontent, thoroughly spelling out French's inadequacies, for which he had garnered much support, when Haig's horse balked and threw his majesty, physically injuring him to the extent that he was laid up in bed for days. As a result, Haig's diary and much of the press affords a disproportionate amount of coverage to this 'catastrophic event'.

Regarding the Loos debacle, Lord Kitchener was rebuked for his support of French needs irrespective of heavy British losses. Sir John French held his reserve troops too far from the front and deployed them too late to exploit the initial success. His plan proved to be entirely different from that which his field commanders had expected, thus vainly sacrificing the initiative and thousands of lives and perhaps the chance of shortening the war. He left France for good in November 1915. Sir Douglas Haig died in January 1928. Ten years later, on the unveiling of his memorial in Whitehall, *The Times* reported:

Of the men who were the nation's leaders, in council or action, twenty years ago, the reputation of none has been allowed to rest unchallenged. It could be otherwise with the actors in such great events; and controversy has not spared the name of Haig. But, largely because he scrupulously and chivalrously refrained from defending himself or accusing others, it has done little or nothing to depreciate his distinction in military history, and has left his personal character wholly untarnished.

A fortnight's battle on the Western Front had cost the Allies as much as nine months in the Dardanelles. Despite the initial optimism expressed with regard to both campaigns, Churchill had disappeared from the Admiralty in May and from the Cabinet in October. Sir John French lost his command of the British forces in December when it became apparent that the war had taken a darker turn. In fairness, even the most brilliant tacticians of the day were the products of a bygone age, lacking the qualities required to fight a more modern war. There were a few exceptions, such as General Thwaites, but overall the expertise was not there for an Allied victory over an enemy that had played a skilful game and won. Dug in as they were and well fortified, the Germans were confident that they could hold their line with inferior numbers against any attack made by the Allied forces. At the same time they believed they could break the strength of Russia and overrun the Balkans. Conceivably the Germans might have done better in 1915 to concentrate on the Western Front, but in all probability they made the right choice. At Loos, the attacking brigade pursued its objectives with guts and determination and in this Rifleman Frank Edwards of 1st Battalion London Irish Rifles played no small part. The act of kicking a football over the top rallied an initiating attack into a cloud of poisonous gas and the horrors beyond. The story of its footballer is very much that of Loos, a forgotten event in a dim and distant battle hurriedly buried as bad news.

The Christmas Truce came about when the war was young and was widely believed to be all over before the New Year. 'There will nothing of that this year', declared *The War Illustrated* in its December 1915 issue. The Germans at many points were anxious to have an informal truce, it claimed. They were already calling out beyond their lines 'Christmas coming. No more shoot.' But they met no response:

> Our armies have too many bitter recollections from the twelve months that have passed. Recollections that cannot be effaced. They have read of the treatment of our own soldiers in German prison camps. They have experienced the German poison gas … There will be no stretching out of friendly hands this year.

Christmas 1915 would be observed in very marked fashion. Unless an advance was ordered, it would be 'quiet along the front'. A signal from GOC 47th (London) Division dated 19 December, reminded all units that a recurrence of the fraternisation would not be tolerated. Lieutenant Colonel Gordon Barber of the 1/Queens Own Cameron Highlanders regretted this. For almost three

64. Sir Douglas Haig.

months after the Battle of Loos had been fought there stretched for 300 yards in front of his trenches the remains of the dead still awaiting burial.

The initial charge of the London Irish at Loos lasted a matter of minutes, as did that of the East Surreys on the Somme ten months later. Whereas the likes of Sir Arthur Conan Doyle immortalised Billie Nevill's footballing adventure, the failure to raise the game at Loos is significant in its absence. The kicking of a football at Loos was more than just another 'agreeable interference' or 'sentimental aside in the dialogue of war', as one anonymous pundit said of the Christmas Truce. Rather it started a battle that was the first indication of how the war was set to continue. Loos was a failure, a mistake, something to be purged from the mind and memory.

The *Weekly Despatch* may or may not have been used to serve the troublesome Irish Question. The culmination of Protestant paranoia, which for centuries found expression in an instinctive anti-Irishness and anti-Catholicism, was still widespread and open to manipulation as a political force. For the duration of the war Irish eyes shined from the pages of the print media to counter German claims of rebellious Irish regiments lurking within the British Army. The lost opportunity to capitalise on the London Irish success at Loos will always remain a mystery and the subsequent reporting of its own the more so. Heroes emerged where they could be found, except for the Footballer of Loos, who should have found a special place. In *Donkeys*, Alan Clark's enduringly controversial account of these chaotic weeks on the Western Front, it is clear that the peoples' perception of Loos bore little resemblance to the reality. In London, Clark records how 'the air was thick with rumour … as the hospital trains rolled into Charing Cross with many of the wounded talking of the impossibility of their task they had been given, of the hopeless sacrifice of comrades'. Henry Williamson's alter-ego, Phillip Maddison, passing by that same railway station, hears a paper boy call out about the new attack on Western Front at Loos. The *Star* reports the excellent morale of the British troops, which to Maddison only belonged in the streets about him and not the hellish reality he had stepped out of.

Loos may never find its rightful place in First World War history. Perhaps it is too late. Had the circumstances been different, then probably Conan Doyle and other commentators would have made as much of the rifleman who kick-started the battle as they did the captain who followed suit on the Somme. Both men played the same game for the same reasons. Billy Nevill died as a result and his sacrifice stands as testimony to the many thousands slaughtered in one day. Frank Edwards lived, but even as his broken body was making its way home, his moment and the battle fought at Loos was fading. His comrades, either wounded or remaining could only have wondered what to tell the folks back home. Were it not for the account in the *Weekly Despatch* then their collective memory would have been as those who witnessed the Christmas Truce, did it happen or was it all imagined?

In *The Great Push*, Patrick MacGill writes that he tried as far as he was allowed to give an account of the attack in which he took part. Practically the whole book was written in the scene of action, and the chapter dealing with the night at Les Brebis, prior to the Big Push, was written in the trench between midnight and dawn of 25 September. The concluding chapter was written in the hospital at Versailles two days after he had been wounded at Loos. With himself cast as the central character, MacGill offers the reader a more authentic experience than Geoffrey Belton Cobb's chronicle of events, which was more compliant to the constraints of the censors. MacGill had lived a previous life on the page as Dermod Flynn, the central character of *Children of the Dead*, a thinly fictionalised account of the hardships he experienced growing up. Clearly his experience of the trenches did not lend themselves to the device of fellow authors filling the shelves of bookshops with jingoistic semi-autobiographical novels.

Captain C. J. C. Street sits somewhere between the two. *With The Guns* is essentially a series of sketches designed to inform the 'average man' as simply as could be put the art of the artilleryman. Street's personal account of his war is typical of the type of material available throughout the conflict. It lays out the case for the ordinary individual finding himself in an extraordinary situation. Alan Clarke was the first military historian to tackle cogently what Liddell Hart first described as the 'unwanted battle' of Loos. Clarke wrote his definitive *The Donkeys* in 1961 and it remained the most influential account until Philip Warner announced in 1973 that 'a great deal of nonsense' had been written about the Battle of Loos, which he set about righting. Personal testimony, where it could be found, was linked to the official histories, which by themselves have proved to be limited.

In the 90th anniversary year of the battle (2005) Niall Cherry's *Most Unfavourable Ground*, followed by Gordon Corrigan's *The Unwanted Battle* (2006) and Nick Lloyd's *Loos 1915* collectively taint Clarke's viewpoint as an unreliable rant against the butchery of the British High Command. Nick Lloyd seeks to distinguish whether the failure of Loos was actually about inexperienced and partly trained officers and men without the proper resources to do the work of soldiers. He alone records of the first day, the 25 September 1915:

> With a favourable wind and good ground, the leading battalion (1/18th London) of 141 Brigade swept over no man's land and was soon upon the German front line, where after a swift fight, most of the bewildered defenders broke and ran. Within ten minutes it was through the first line of trenches, and had been 'leapfrogged' by the two supporting battalions (1/19th and 1/20th London), which continued the advance.

Reviewing those two sentences with the benefit of what other evidence can be found beyond the official sources neatly encapsulates the problem of anyone attempting to compile a defining history of Loos. Bad leadership or luck, or something in between, the first four days of the Battle of Loos is bare on the page without the inclusion of the actions of Thwaites' 141st Brigade. As war correspondent Philip Gibbs put it:

> … never a battalion broke in mutiny against inevitable martyrdoms. Their discipline did not break. However profound was the despair of the individual, the mass moved as it was directed from one shambles to another with the same valour that prevailed and uplifted.

Observing the assault as he did, C. J. C. Street makes the point:

> … the facts so far as known – and no two accounts, even of those who took part in the struggle, quite agree – are as follows: The 47th Division, London Territorials all of them, the heroes of the day, but of whose performances, because less showy, little has been heard, had by 9.30am surmounted a series of obstacles, the storming of any one of which would have earned them lasting fame.

As Nick Lloyd has it, 'notwithstanding the mixed success of the opening assault' the 'excellent' artillery preparations had allowed 15th and 47th Divisions to make major gains and provide the battle with 'perhaps its most famous episode' in the form of the 15th Scottish Division's taking of Hill 70. There was no such recorder documenting the lead battalion at Loos, only those that were there and who lived to tell the tale.

As part of a talk to a meeting of the Henry Williamson Society in November 2005, entitled 'The Literary Alchemy of the Battle of Loos', Ian Walker revealed that he had made the connection with Captain Street and Phillip Maddison in Williamson's fictional war novel, *A Fox Under My Cloak*, said to contain a 'totally convincing description' of the Battle of Loos. Williamson is applauded as a rare recorder of the suburban English social structure as it was before the First World War and one who offers 'a more accurate view of Edwardian society than any retrospective scholastic social history'. Williamson is also credited as one who reflects a more genuine view of the horrors of war than those who had never experienced the rough brutalities of life. He never fought at Loos but lent heavily on the official history of the war, believing it to be the definitive account, and also looked to C. J. C. Street for authentic material in order to tell as true a story about the war as he could.

The closest Williamson comes to any acknowledgement of the London Territorials at Loos is a reference to the assaulting troops withdrawn to rehearse the attack. In *Tales of a Devon Village: Cemetery or Burial Ground*, Williamson balances the view that Loos failed as a result of the wrong kind of shells. By recognising that the reasons were far more complex than that, they 'absolutely did not include a failure by the Generals to plan for the battle'.

History is a thorny preoccupation at the best of times, more often fuelling cynicism or fanning the flames of discontent than offering satisfaction. 'Command and Control in 1915 – the attack on Lone Tree, 25 September 1915' was an article published in 2006 in *Stand To!*, the journal of the Western Front Association. Based on an extract from his PhD thesis, Nick Lloyd criticises Williamson's 'compelling and dramatic' rendition of Loos as 'not entirely accurate', taking issue with the novelist's criticism of what he calls the 'criminal stupidity of the orders of British command'. Lloyd's singling out of Williamson on this point was met with fierce defence in the form of a letter and then a full response published in the *Henry Williamson Society Journal* entitled 'The Spectre of Lone Tree'. Whereas Lloyd claims the reasons for the failure at Loos were uncut wire, problems with gas dispersal and chaotic communications, Williamson does likewise in his novel but, as his supporters have it, 'with an excellent grasp of battle necessity'.

In another much earlier lecture about Loos and its implications for future operations, Rawlinson's Chief of Staff at IV Corps, Brigadier-General A. A. Montgomery, commended the attack of the 47th (London) Division, but noted that its mission was 'far easier' than the tasks allotted other divisions deployed further north which had to make all-out attacks. The failure of the all-out attack, Montgomery added, did not 'prove that it was a mistake'. It failed because of a 'faulty method of execution' and not the selection of the 'wrong form of objective'. Williamson's Phillip Maddison attends a similar lecture given by a war correspondent, a lunchtime affair on The *Opening Phases of the Battle of Loos*. The lecturer stands by a blackboard upon which are chalked various diagrams. He is nervous and can hardly be heard, despite the calls for him to speak up. Eventually the lecture ends and the speaker calls out:

> Gentlemen, I feel I must ask your indulgence for what must appear, to many of you who had to do the fighting, a most imperfect account of it. I do assure you all that I, as a mere distant spectator, feel most humble when I think of what you were called upon to do – and what you did was magnificent. Our great national poet Shakespeare said that the world was a stage. This remark has never been more fully illustrated in all our island story than in the past two weeks. You, gentlemen, are the actors; we who stand and wait are but the audience…

Ending with the problems of reporters in the rear acting as a clearing-place of often contrary messages and reports, he concludes that

> … only gradually can the whole picture of what is happening be built up. Thus in one sector all may seem, for the time being, to be lost; while that aspect, by its very pessimism, may enable troops a mile away to overcome the enemy position and so effect a break in his defences.

The lecturer pauses to a dead silence, claiming he had done his best to give an outline of the three days of battle. His request for questions is finally answered with 'a curt growl':

> The other day I took part in the battle of Loos. Now, having listened to the lecturer, he has proved to me that I was never there. I would like to ask 'im to explain that.

The marquee filled with laughter, cheering and clapping and the meeting broke up.

★ ★ ★

Loos, City of the Dead! If in years to come you are ever rebuilt, a task that to the observer of your utter destruction and desolation seems impossible, what strange and gruesome relics will your workmen find! Surely the Spirit of Carnage will for ever haunt those narrow streets and open wide-spread fields, surely your inhabitants of the future will wake in terror in the September nights to hear ghostly echoes of the then-forgotten struggle, the unceasing whistle and roar of the shells, the rushing footsteps of the charging men, the despairing cries of the bombed wretches in the cellars! And, if timid eyes dare lift the curtain to peep fearfully through the windows, will they not see a blood-red moon shining upon the streets through which pour the serried columns of the victors, and scent the night air tainted with a faint sickening odour of slaughter? But not alone shall Loos bear its burden of horror, for in how many towns and villages must these scenes be repeated before Peace comes again?

Captain C. J. C. Street OBE, MC. Royal Garrison Artillery Special Reserve. 1916

The town of Loos-en-Gohelle has been rebuilt, created out of a demand in France for the return of lost heritage following the massive destruction of the First World War. In this, regionalism became the principle guideline for reconstruction in the devastated regions. Shunned by the modernists, regionalism was similar to the arts and crafts movement in stressing craftsmanship over the uniformity and loss of quality in industrial production. Loos exemplifies this heritage factor in its traditional architecture and building materials, for without any knowledge of its violent past, the casual passer-by might be forgiven for believing that the town had escaped the worst horrors of the 1914–18 war. But then this is a place that attracts few casual passers-by. There are no hotels or guest houses. Loos-en-Gohelle is a working town, not a tourist destination. Dominated by mountains of industrial spoil straddling vast flat agricultural plains, those visitors that do come are invariably drawn by the ghosts of their ancestors.

Whereas the centuries-old rooflines and weathered brick walls cunningly deceive the eye, the town hall looks a product of heritage architecture but is no less splendid for that. It is here that the *Sur les traces de la Grande Guerre* (On thes Trail of the Great War) Association has set up the Loos battlefield Museum. Formed in 1992 as a result of the continued interest in the First World War, the core objectives of the Association are to preserve the memory of the conflict and to conserve what of it survives.

When my wife and I visited the town, our guide for the tour was Alfred Duparcq, the ardent President of the Association. His English is as rare as my French, but that was irrelevant as he took my wife's arm to lead her to a reproduction of Lady Butler's *An Image of Loos* presented to the museum by the London Irish Rifles Regimental Association. Born Elizabeth Thompson

65. Loos laid low.

and most famous for 'Roll Call', painted in 1874, popular support for Lady Butler's paintings waned because of her strong opinions about the suffering of Catholics in Ireland. She continued to paint military pictures until her death in 1933 but never again enjoyed the popularity of her early career. *An Image of Loos* was painted in 1916 and presented to the London Irish Rifles Regimental Association.

'*Grandpere?*' quizzed Monsieur Duparcq, pointing to the young Tommy pictured kicking a football ahead of the charge. '*Oui*' Sue replied, bringing out of her bag a photograph of herself as a six-year-old with her mother and the man himself. It came as a revelation that a name could be attached to the footballer and that he had survived. Monsieur Duparcq's astonishment grew as I drew out of my folder photographs and press cuttings following the trail of the Footballer of Loos. Smartly ushered into another exhibition area, a gesticulating finger hovered over the British line set out on a large battlefield map hanging on the wall, accompanied by a repetitive, 'football?' I placed my own finger midfield of the plain directly north of Rue Jules Supervielle, facing due east in the direction of the D943 Route de Bethune. Transposing the 1915 trench map with a modern day Blue Series gives the position of the 18th London facing the spur of Rue de Supervielle with Chemin de Mazingarbe. Monsieur Duparcq smiled, declaring he knew the place well.

The 1915 trench map defines the formation of the 47th Division with the London regiments spread as far south as the modern day A21 Autoroute.

66. An Image of Loos. (Courtesy of the London Irish Rifles Regimental Association)

67. The footprints of 'Tower Bridge'.

Although positioned forward along the entire length of the planned assault on Loos, there is little or no reference to the Londoners in the Loos museum. The London Irish have established their place, but otherwise the story of Loos lies predominately with the Scots and the Canadians. From the French perspective, however, it is important to remember that there were three major battles fought here. The first battle took place on 9 May 1915 and saw the massacre of two French regiments. The second, which began on 25 September 1915, is the one better known to the British as 'The Battle of Loos', and the third began on the 15 August 1917 where the Canadians were instrumental in removing the last vestiges of German occupation. Just as the kicking of the football might be regarded as emblematic of the first Big Push, so the museum is symbolic of the region's place in the First World War.

After lunch we duly reported back to the museum as instructed where Monsieur Duparcq was waiting to take us to the spot where Frank kicked off his football. First we stopped at a recreation ground on the southern outskirts of the town, once the site of the mighty pit pylons known to the Londoners as Tower Bridge, and now reduced to concrete footsteps in the grass.

Pausing briefly at St. Patrick's Cemetery, we drove past the house of Emilienne Moreau, 'The Lady of Loos' who saved a British soldier and armed with explosives helped force the Germans from their stronghold and later shooting two more. For her bravery she was awared the Croix de Guerre 1914–1918, the Croix du Combattant, the Military Medal, the Red Cross (first class) and the Venerable Order of Saint John, and was later invited to meet the President of the French Republic and King George V.

Just as Captain Street had predicted, across the whole expansion and redevelopment of Loos-en-Gohelle, many a strange and gruesome relic is revealed almost on a daily basis by workmen. The line where the London Irish were dug in is entered along a narrow path cut sometime after 1918 across the field which was just as we expected it to be, a pitilessly flat ground with no mercy from the biting wind or the icy rain, let alone a relentless hail machine-gun fire. All that remains of the line is a slight ridge scarring the ground from north to south. An unexploded shell protruding from the mud by the roadside was a rusting reminder of the great artillery barrage. With layers of the thick sticky mud clinging to our boots with each step, we came to a spot close enough to call where the football was sent flying into the wall of poison gas and high velocity ammunition. To the south, somewhere in the smoke and gloom the Double Crassier dominated the skyline as it does now, offering a distinct disadvantage to the advancing 6th and 7th London regiments. Then a slug-like edifice trailing down half a kilometre from the Rue de Ragonieux, the twin peaks would have only just caught the corner of Frank's eye as he raced forward. Now they have contracted, expanded and risen to form the largest pair of slag heaps in Europe.

68. Emilienne
Moreau.

69. The field of play.

70. The Loos Memorial at Dud Corner.

Frank fell before reaching the German line, his comrades surging on. Having taken their objective they pushed forward towards Loos Cemetery, now three times the size it was in 1915, and then on into Loos, to hold the line against all the odds until the reinforcements finally arrived days later. This story of Loos is never told. The 47th Division's bitter struggle has left few footprints in the reading of the first fruitless encounter on the Western Front.

The Loos Memorial at Dud Corner is located on the site of the Lens Road Redoubt, a large German defensive position attacked and captured by the 9th (Scottish) Division on the first day of the Battle of Loos. From the few burials here in 1918 it has grown to commemorate the 20,633 soldiers who were killed in the Loos sector from 25 September 1915 until October 1918 and who have no known graves. The majority of the stones that bear names are those of the men who fell in the Battle of Loos, with seemingly every regiment of the British Army represented. The names most often mentioned in despatches are those of Lieutenant John Kipling, the poet Charles Hamilton Sorley and the late Queen Mother's brother, Captain Fergus Bowes-Lyon.

The final resting place of Rudyard Kipling's son, John, lay undiscovered for 77 years, despite the famous writer's desperate searching. Then in 1992, in a highly unusual move, the Commonwealth War Graves Commission re-marked the grave of an unknown lieutenant of the Irish Guards as that of John Kipling. However, in November 2007 the Imperial War Museum mounted an exhibition covering John Kipling's life, including the naming of another candidate for the body identified by the War Graves Commission. The subsequent play and book about John (or Jack) Kipling's short life makes no claim to be a documentary account, but a representation of the experience of so many families who lost sons during the war.

Compared to the battlefields of the Somme and Ypres this is a place too often overlooked by military historians, yet it represents the most important actions of the early war with arguably a profound effect on its subsequent course. The Dud Memorial, as one of the highest concentration of military cemeteries along the Western Front, bears witness to the comparatively few visitors this area receives.

The name 'Dud Corner' is said to be derived from the large number of unexploded enemy shells uncovered after 1918. At the back, or north east, wall of the enclosure towers the Cross of Sacrifice, which lies central to four open circular courts. On the high walls leading back to the front end of the cemetery on the Route to Bethune are hung the stone tablets onto which are carved the names of those commemorated. The southern wall faces the direction of the attacking division of the 141st Infantry Brigade, where the tablets contain the names of the postmen, the civil servants, the artists and artisans of the 47th London volunteers whose success at Loos awaits the wider recognition it so richly deserves.

Postscript

When Frank Edwards died in 1964, tributes paid to him in local and national newspapers commemorated the passing of the man they called the Footballer of Loos. 'I was not surprised when I heard what he had done' his daughter Daphne told reporters, 'He was a lovable man but fearless.' His son, Frank, proudly recalled his father re-enacting his exploit at Loos and how he attended the London Irish Rifles' centenary celebrations in 1959. Probably as a result of his BBC broadcast in 1935, Frank was offered employment as a timekeeper at a Maidenhead factory, which held the promise of paid security for the remainder of his working life. Back in 1929 he had re-enlisted in the Military Police to bring about his maximum 21 years army service. With only a few months to go before reaching the full term, he decided to take the gamble and accept the job and was granted his discharge on 4 December 1935.

Unfortunately the position fell through shortly afterwards and a series of temporary jobs followed. On 27 October 1937 Frank began a probationary training period with the National Society for the Prevention of Cruelty to Children (NSPCC). Five months later he became an inspector and moved with his family to the NSPCC Central Glamorgan local office in Bridgend, South Wales, which covered a large area, making good use of Frank's motorcycle training with the Military Police. Fast earning a reputation as a much-respected inspector, his new career was interrupted on recall to the Army on 31 August 1939 at the outbreak of war for the second time in his life. At 43 years of age, however, and because of the job he was doing, Frank was returned a month later to the NSPCC.

Just before Christmas 1943 he decided to quit the service and return to war-torn London, leaving the NSPCC against the backdrop of much praise from local magistrates, court officials, the police and solicitors for the manner in which he dealt with cases of child cruelty brought before the courts. His last

71. Frank Edwards, his daughter, Daphne and granddaughter, Susan.

72. The Loos Football, 2008.

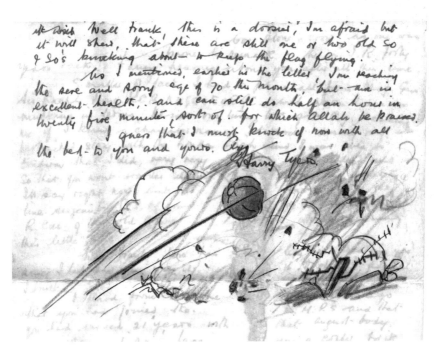

73. Harry Tyers' illustrated letter.

plea was for leniency to be shown towards a mother who had been summoned for neglecting her two children.

Frank Edwards and his family then moved to a pleasant mid-nineteenth century villa facing Twickenham Green, west of London. He worked variously as a swimming instructor, an office manager at a local bakery and then a Teddington engineering firm. In 1957, a year after his wife died, Frank came to stay with his daughter, Daphne, who lived close by the Royal Military School of Music in Whitton, where Frank had been a batman for a time. Both of Frank Edwards' children have now passed away. His grandson, William, lives in France and his granddaughter Susan lives in the house in Whitton where he died. Susan recalls a large, affable man who liked his beer. When he lived off Twickenham Green, Frank's dog, Tigg, would be sent to the pub to retrieve him when it was time for dinner. In later life he was greeted on his return by his budgie, Joey, who managed to escape his cage only once, the day that Frank died peacefully in his armchair.

In the 90th anniversary year of the Battle of Loos in 2005, the Royal Military Police Roll of Honour lists Frank Edwards as 'The Mad Footballer of Loos, WWI'. On its website, D Company, The London Regiment (London Irish Rifles) celebrates the 1st Battalion's distinguished exploit at the Battle of Loos 'led by the captain of the football team, Sgt Edwards, who took his football and kicked it towards the objective'. But the ambiguity endures. Each year on Loos Sunday, it is the charge that it is commemorated and not the individual, which is probably how Frank would want it. During the move from Chelsea to Camberwell, the London Irish Rifles Regimental Museum lost its erstwhile curator through illness, leaving the legend of the Footballer even more disjointed. Despite curator Bert Coward's vigorous views expressed in 1964 regarding who was the Footballer of Loos was, the odd newspaper clipping survives in the new museum reporting Edwards' death. The fading exhibit tag once attaching the ball lies in a drawer and the football itself, now deflated and torn, occupies a place of honour in the officer's mess.

As well as the Prussian officer's sword Frank 'borrowed from the Kaiser's Palace', his medals, a few trappings from his time in the Military Police and the small collection of crumbling newspaper clippings preserved by his granddaughter, one piece of correspondence survives in the form of an illustrated letter from the celebrated Harry Tyers. Before its move from the Duke of York's Headquarters, Chelsea, the walls of the London Irish Rifles Regimental HQ were awash with many of these wonderfully illustrated letters produced by the regiment's consummate caricaturist correspondent. The letter to Frank Edwards concludes with the sketch of a football under fire flying over the line.

Sources and Bibliography

Archival

Imperial War Museum

Acc No: S.6/773: Aldershot Command Searchlight Tattoo: Official Souvenir. Gale &
    Polden 1926. Acc No. S.6/825: Southern Command Searchlight Tattoo: Tidworth.
    Official Programme. Fleetway Press. 1926. ID No. 52532: Great Torchlight &
    Searchlight Tattoo. Stadium, Wembley. (No Date). Acc No. S.80/39: S.S.A.F.A
    Searchlight Tattoo at White City Stadium 1952.
Souvenir in aid of St Dunstan's Hostel.
Acc. 97/295: The London Irish Rifles: The 1/18th Battalion London Regiment: War
    History 1914–1919. Compiled by 2nd Lt. S F Major. NP 1996.
Sons of Victory 1914–1918. Alan Nichols. 1935.

Hammersmith & Fulham Archive

Earls Court and Olympia: From Buffalo Bill to The 'Brits'. John Glanfield. Sutton. 2003.
    Olympia. A souvenier Review Commemorating The Golden Jubilee 1887–1937.
    Editor Felix Brittain. Officially authorised by Olympia Ltd. 1937. Ed.S. Borrow &
    Co. Ltd.
The Souless Stadium – A Memoir of London's White City (A 3–2 Sporting Retrospective)
    by Fred H. Hawthorn and Ronald Price. 3–2 Books, 2001.

Newspapers and Periodicals

Daily Sketch, 25 November 1915
Daily Sketch, 18 March 1916
The Daily Telegraph, 25 February 2006
Dublin Mail, 16 November 1915

Emerald: The Journal of the London Irish, No 62. 2005

Evening News, (London) 27 September 1915, 1925–22 September 1926, 25 September 1935, p.11, 16 November 1959, p.8

Evening News & Star, (London) 27 January 1964

Evening Standard, 14 February 1966

The *Guardian*, 25 March 1998, 24 December 2001, 10 September 2004

Henry Williamson Society Journal, No.43, September 2007

Illustrated London News, 16 December 1914, 9 October 1915, 30 October 1915 1915, 25 December 1915, 8 January 1916

Irish Times, 21 July 1931, 1 August 1931

Lloyd's Weekly News, 29 August 1915

London Gazette, October 26, 1915, 1/16/18 November 1915

Morning Post, 24 November 1915

The *Newbury Herald*, 1935

News of the World, 2 February 1964

Surrey Mirror, 2 March 1915

Thames Valley Times, January 1964

The *Times*, 11 November 1937

The War Illustrated, Vol.3. J.A. Hammerton (ed) Amalgamated Press

The War Illustrated, 16 January 1915, 31 July 1915, 9 October 1915, 16 October 1915

Weekly Despatch, 31 October 1915

West London Observer, 3 July 1925

West London Press, 24 September 1926

World War 1914–1918: A Pictured History, Sir John Hammerton (Ed). Amalgamated Press, 1935

Maps

Map of Battle Area, 1915

The London Territorials, 1915

Published Sources

Arthur, Max, *Forgotten Voices of The Great War* (Ebury Press, 2003)

Bowman, Timothy, *Irish Regiments in the Great War – Discipline and Morale* (Manchester University Press, 2003)

Brown, Malcolm & Shirley Seaton, *Christmas Truce* (Pan Books, 2001)

Chappell, Mike, *REDCAPS, Britain's Military Police* (Osprey, 1997)

Cherry, Niall, *Most Unfavourable Ground: The Battle of Loos 1915* (Helion & Company, 2005)

Clark, Alan, *The Donkeys* (Pimlico, 1993)

Cobb, G., *Stand to Arms* (Wells Gardner, Darton & Co Ltd. 1916)

Corbally, M. J. P. M., *London Irish Rifles, 1859–1959: The Regimental Centenary* (The Paramount Press, 1959)

Corrigan, Gordon, *Loos 1915 – The Unwanted Battle* (Spellmount, 2005)

Edmonds, James E., *History of the Great War based on Official Documents Committee of Imperial Defence* (Department of Printed Books, Imperial War Museum, 1995)

Foreman, Michael, *War Game* (Arcade, 1994)

Fussell, Paul, *The Great War and Modern Memory* (Oxford University Press, 1977)

Gavaghan, Michael, *An Illustrated Pocket Guide to the Battle of Loos, 1915* (M and L Publications, 1997)

Gibbs, Philip, *The Soul of War* (Heinemann, 1915)

Gledhill, Christine, *Reframing British Cinema, 1918–1928: Between Restraint and Passion* (BFI Publishing, 2003)

Hall, James Norman, *Kitchener's Mob* (Houghton Mifflin, 1916)

Harris, Clive and Whippy, Julian, *The Greater Game: Sporting Icons who fell in the Great War* (Pen and Sword, 2008)

Jack, Alexander, *McCrae's Battalion* (Mainstream Publishing, 2003)

Lloyd, Nick, *Loos 1915* (Tempus Publishing, 2006)

Lord Fraser of Lonsdale, *My Story of St Dunstan's* (Harrap, 1961)

Low, Rachel, *The History of British Film Vol.4* (Routledge, 1996)

Manchester, William, *The Last Lion: Winston Spencer Churchill Visions of Glory 1874–1932* (Sphere Books Ltd. 1984)

Maude, Alan H. (Ed), *History of the 47th (London) Division 1914–1919* (Naval & Military Books, reprinted 2002)

May, Ernest, *Signal Corporal: The Story of the 2nd Battalion London Irish Rifles (2/18th Battalion London Regiment) 1914–1918* (Johnson Publications, 1972)

McGill, Patrick, *The Amateur Army* (Herbert Jenkins, 1915)

McGill, Patrick, *The Great Push* (Herbert Jenkins, 1916)

Middlebrook, Martin, *The First Day on the Somme: 1 July 1916* (Penguin, 1984)

Pearson, Sir Arthur, *Victory over Blindness* (Hodder & Stoughton, 1919)

Pollard, A. F., *A Short History of The Great War* (Methuen & Co. 1919)

Stannard, Paul, *They Took the Lead* (DDP One Stop UK Ltd, 1998)

Street, Capt. C. J. C., *With the Guns* (Naval & Military Press, 2005)

Warner, Philip, *The Battle of Loos* (William Kimber & Co. 1976 r/p Wordsworth Editions Ltd. 2000)

Williamson, Henry, *A Fox Under My Cloak* (Sutton Publishing, 1996: vol. 5 of *A Chronicle of Ancient Sunlight*)

Unpublished and Online Sources

Bourne, John, 'Hon Edward James Montagu-Stuart-Wortley, Major-General CB CMG MVO DSO. GOC Infantry Division, Eton College. King's Royal Rifle Corps' Centre for First World War Studies

Nobbs, Stuart David, 'British Participation in the Battle of Loos, 25 September – 13 October 1915: A Re-evaluation' (www.leeds.ac.uk/history/studentlife/e-journal/Nobbs.pdf)

http://www.firstworldwar.bham.ac.uk/donkey/wortley.htm

www.1914–1918.net/frenchs_ninth_despatch.htm

Index

74. Frank Edwards' granddaughter Susan Harris holding the Loos football, 2009.